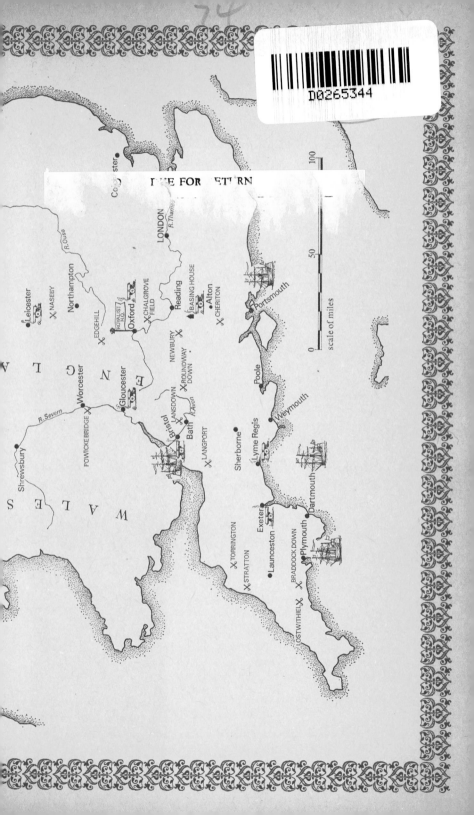

KING CHARLES,
PRINCE RUPERT,
AND THE CIVIL WAR

KING CHARLES, PRINCE RUPERT, AND THE CIVIL WAR

FROM ORIGINAL LETTERS

EDITED BY

Sir Charles Petrie

Bt, CBE, FRHist.S, Hon.DPhil (Valladolid),
Hon.LittD (National University of Ireland) MA (Oxon),
Corresponding Member
of the Royal Spanish Academy of History,
President of the Military History Society of Ireland

Routledge & Kegan Paul
London

First published in 1974
by Routledge & Kegan Paul Ltd
Broadway House, 68–74 Carter Lane,
London EC4V 5EL
Set in 'Monotype' Walbaum
and printed in Great Britain by
W & J Mackay Limited, Chatham
ISBN 0 7100 7969 9

CONTENTS

PREFACE

The genesis of this book is due to the public spirit of Colonel Alan
Dower, TD, DL, in whose possession is the bulk of the letters
upon which it is based. Those connected with the Royalist party
formed a portion of the correspondence of Prince Rupert which
was transmitted from generation to generation by his secretary to their descendant Mr Bennetts of Pyt House in Wilt-
shire, who was at one time MP for South Wilts. By him they
were sold in 1847 to Mr Bentley, the publisher, who placed them
in the hands of Mr Eliot Warburton, the editor of *The Memoirs
of Prince Rupert and the Cavaliers*.

The history of the Fairfax and other letters connected with the
side of the Parliament is more romantic. The Fairfaxes originated
at Denton in Yorkshire, and during the eighteenth century one
of its members intermarried with the Martins of Leeds Castle,
Kent. In 1822 the Martin of the day had occasion to make some
alterations to the castle, and he set aside for sale a quantity of
furniture for which he had no further use, and among it was an
old oak chest filled with Dutch tiles: this was purchased by a
shoemaker in the neighbouring village of Lenham for a mere
trifle; but under the tiles were found, carefully arranged, the

Fairfax correspondence, which the worthy shoemaker regarded as waste paper and consigned to the cellar for destruction as occasion might require. At this point the matter came to the ears of a banker in Maidstone, who took the necessary steps to preserve the documents, but not before some of them had been cut into strips for the shoemaker's purposes. In due course Mr Bentley purchased this collection, too, and it figured in *The Fairfax Correspondence* which was edited by Messrs Robert Bell and George W. Johnson.

Eventually both collections passed into the possession of Lord Overstone, and then into that of Colonel Alan Dower, who bought them at Sotheby's, being a keen student of the Civil War.

The letters have now been edited with a view to throwing the maximum amount of light upon the personalities of their writers, and for this reason others from different collections have been included for the purpose of clarification: with the same end in view a certain amount of historical and personal background has been painted in. It is hoped that as a result the Civil War will be seen in its proper perspective through the eyes of those who participated in it.

The letters of King Charles I and King Charles II being Crown Copyright, I have to express my gratitude to Her Majesty the Queen for her gracious permission to publish them. It is also at once a pleasure and a duty to express my grateful thanks to Colonel Dower for his unfailing kindness and assistance on all occasions: he has rendered the writing of this book one of the most delightful of tasks.

CHARLES PETRIE

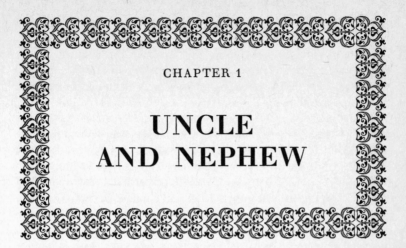

CHAPTER 1

UNCLE AND NEPHEW

The character of the Civil War is often misunderstood. Those whose sympathies are with the Parliament not infrequently regard the struggle as one between a faithless and tyrannical monarch, backed by a loose-living aristocracy, on the one hand, and a sober and liberty-loving middle class on the other. On the contrary, those who incline towards the royal cause are apt to see the conflict in the light of a conspiracy by a minority of determined revolutionaries, prepared to stop at nothing to achieve their nefarious purpose. Too often the pen and the brush have depicted the Civil War in one or other of these strong lights, and very rarely has it been shown in those half-tones which more nearly approximate to the truth. From the beginning there were certainly many who had no doubt which side they would espouse if and when the sword was drawn, but there must have been far more who hesitated until the last moment. The issue was not at the beginning so clear cut as it became later, or as it appears in retrospect, when much is obvious that was hidden from contemporaries: nor did it remain unchanged from the meeting of the Long Parliament to the Restoration of Charles II. Many thought that enough had been done when the Prerogative Courts were abolished;

1

more were alienated from the Parliamentary cause when the King was beheaded; and only a remnant was satisfied to see the hereditary monarchy replaced by a military dictatorship. So it came about that no inconsiderable proportion of those who had opposed Charles I were quite genuine in welcoming the return of his son.

To the historian in his study two or three centuries later, with all the relevant documents at his disposal, it may appear strange that men should have had any hesitation in declaring for one side or the other, but to take such a view is surely to betray ignorance of human nature. When the dynastic crisis first burst upon the British Empire in December 1936, and before it was realized exactly what was at stake, men and women who had many beliefs in common suddenly found themselves taking diametrically opposite views: so it was in 1641 with much more reason. Thousands of swords must have been drawn for King or Parliament only with the greatest reluctance, and this may well explain the relative mildness of the struggle compared with the horrors of the contemporary Thirty Years' War. Kipling described the situation very well when he wrote of the battle of Edgehill:

> But there is no change as we meet at last
> On the brow-head or the plain,
> And the raw astonished ranks stand fast
> To slay or to be slain
> By the men they knew in the kindly past
> That shall never come again—
>
> By the men they met at dance or chase,
> In the tavern or the hall,
> At the justice-bench and the market place
> At the cudgel-play or brawl,
> Of their own blood and speech and race
> Comrades or neighbours all!

In effect, whichever side one believes to have been in the right, one cannot shut one's eyes to the fact that there were honest men on the other, as well as fools and knaves, and that for many of our ancestors the choice must have been very difficult indeed. Typical of the attitude of many must have been that of the Roundhead Waller who wrote to the Cavalier Hopton, 'The Great God, Who is the searcher of my heart, knows with what reluctance I go upon this service, and with what perfect hatred I look upon a war without an enemy.'

The conduct of the war, with which we are primarily concerned in these pages, at any rate in England itself though certainly not in Ireland, or where the Irish were concerned, was on the whole merciful, and in this the King set a notable example. There were often relatives on both sides, as at the siege of Sherborne Castle, where the daughter-in-law of its defender was the sister of the Parliamentary commander who besieged it. She told her brother that if he were determined to reduce the place he 'should find his sister's bones buried in the ruins'; whereupon he raised the siege. A further illustration is afforded by an episode which occurred in 1645 after Cromwell's capture of Winchester. The prisoners complained of being robbed contrary to the terms of surrender. Six men in particular were accused, and Cromwell had them put on trial: all were found guilty, one chosen by lot was hanged, and five were sent to the Royalist governor at Oxford, who returned them 'with an acknowledgement of the Lieutenant-General's nobleness'.

Such behaviour was very different from the savagery which had marked the previous civil contest, namely the Wars of the Roses. The combatants in that struggle were professional soldiers, bred in the hard school of the French wars; as the late Professor Mowat wrote:

> Troops of men, nobles, mercenary captains, common soldiers, came back into England, demoralized by long years of bitter warfare, of fighting for their lives and their booty amid an alien people. War was their only occupation. In time of peace they were out of place. For law they had little respect, and the renewal of fighting was their main chance of success.

In the war between Charles and the Parliament, on the other hand, at any rate in its earlier stages, save for a few officers with Continental experience, both armies were composed of amateurs to whom the shedding of blood was a regrettable necessity.

The chief exception on the Royalist side was Prince Rupert of the Rhine, the third son of the Elector Palatine and Elizabeth Stuart, daughter of James I, and consequently the nephew of Charles I. He was only twenty-three when he became involved in the Civil War at his uncle's request, but he had already seen service in Germany, where he had had the misfortune to be taken prisoner by the Imperialists in an action at Vlotho on the Weser, after which he spent several years as a prisoner at Linz. English politics meant nothing to Rupert, who never understood the hesitations which in so many cases accompanied the outbreak of hostilities, and he could not share the horror of Falkland and all the more moderate Cavaliers at the prospect of fighting against Englishmen, for he was not an Englishman but a foreigner and a professional soldier. He was thus liable to commit extremely tactless acts, such as his behaviour at Leicester at the beginning of the war, when he sent a terse note to the Mayor demanding £2,000 on behalf of his uncle. The demand showed a lack of tact, for while most of the leading citizens of Leicester were for the Parliament, there was also a strong party for the King, and the Mayor was himself sitting on the fence, but it seemed perfectly natural to Rupert to raise some money in this way if he could. The upshot is not uninteresting, for the Mayor handed over £500 to keep him quiet, and then sent a galloper to Charles at Nottingham telling him what had happened, whereupon the King promptly repudiated in rather severe language the action of 'my said nephew'.

Uncle and nephew were in fact utterly dissimilar in temperament, and it has been suggested that this may have been the secret of their friendship. Rupert had the greatest respect for the King, but he could never understand in any man a refusal to face facts, especially military facts, yet this is what Charles seemed to him to be doing to an increasing extent as the war progressed, and turned against him. It would be hard to imagine any attitude of mind more opposed to Rupert's practical temperament: his uncle seemed to him to be living in another world. Yet there was in the royal character a core of steel upon which misfortune could not make the slightest impression. He was, before anything else, a man of principle. He had not drawn the sword at Nottingham in any light-hearted mood, but on a point of principle, and while that remained in doubt he would never willingly sheath it. Military defeats were unfortunate and regrettable, but they could not settle the real issue. Charles was always looking for a moral victory, and it can hardly be denied that he got his moral victory in the end, though at the price of his own life.

In no way is the character of the King more clearly revealed, or the contrast between it and that of Rupert more clearly stressed, than in their attitude towards their enemies. For example, Hyde is found writing to Falkland from Oxford under date of 29 September 1642:

> Mr. Hampden[1] and Mr. Goodwyn[2] are at their houses, and our cavalry here think it a very easy matter to take them. His Majesty will give such directions either to those forces which are near those parts, or to their lordships here what shall be done. It is a pity the gentlemen should not be visited.

They were not, however, kidnapped but, on the contrary, when Hampden was mortally wounded on Chalgrove Field, Charles sent his own chaplain to his deathbed. It is difficult to imagine Rupert neglecting such an opportunity.

A further instance of the King's attitude towards his opponents is to be found in his letter to the Mayor of Newbury on 21 September of the following year, and the day after the second battle at that place:

> Our will and command is, that you forthwith send into the towns and villages adjacent, and bring thence all the sick and hurt soldiers of the Earl of Essex's army, and though they be rebels, and deserve the punishment of traitors, yet out of our tender compassion upon them as being our subjects, our will and pleasure is, that you carefully provide for their recovery, as well as for those of our own army, and then to send them to Oxford.

Charles has been accused of trickery, though whether on this score he is any more vulnerable than his opponents is a matter of opinion, but he certainly showed a respect for legality as, for example, when he wrote to the Governor of Dartmouth on 13 December 1643:

> Whereas divers ships and vessels of good value are brought in, as we understand, to our port of Dartmouth, which our and other ships have taken from the rebels and their adherents; and whereas it is like that many more will be hereafter brought in

[1] Of Ship Money fame.
[2] A leading Parliamentarian in Bucks.

thither, concerning which it is fit that there be a legal
proceeding before they be in any way disposed of. Our
pleasure and command therefore is, that you take effectual
order that not only the said ships already brought in, but all
that shall be hereafter, be first legally adjudicated by the judge
of our Admiralty there who is or shall be for the time being,
before you or any others whatsoever, offer to dispose of such
ships, vessels, and prizes, or anything belonging to them, or
any of their goods, and commodities aboard. Which rule we
will and command you punctually to observe and cause to be
observed for the avoiding of injustice, and the prejudice that
would ensue to our service by the contrary.

That Charles should have adopted such a moderate attitude towards his enemies is evidence of that complexity of his character
which was the despair of his contemporaries and has been the
puzzle of posterity. Whereas Rupert saw the Civil War as a war
like any other, his uncle saw it as a crusade and, as we shall see,
this difference in outlook was to cause a rift between them. The
King's chief defect as a ruler and as a commander in the field was
a fatal irresolution and lack of self-confidence, which Rupert
found exasperating. Gardiner, the historian, treated him as a
stupid man, but this was not the opinion of his contemporaries.
Clarendon wrote that 'he had an excellent understanding, but was
not confident enough of it; which made him often-times change
his own opinion for a worse, and follow the advice of a man that
did not judge so well as himself'. His opponent, St John, held much
the same view, and Cromwell went so far as to say that if the
King had trusted his own judgment he would have fooled them
all. This was very marked when war came, and Clarendon put it
on record that 'he was very fearless in his person, but not enterprising'.

There is nothing in the correspondence between uncle and
nephew prior to Rupert's surrender of Bristol in 1645 to indicate
that there were any serious differences between them: even the
defeats of Marston Moor and Naseby had had no adverse effect
upon their relations, which had always been exceptionally cordial.
Almost the only occasion when they seem to have differed was
after Edgehill which, although a drawn battle, could in Rupert's
opinion have been converted into a victory had it been properly

followed up. According to his diary, Rupert 'offered to push on with the horse and three thousand foot; to seize Westminster and the rebel part of the Parliament, and occupy the palace of White-hall until the King should come up with the remainder of the army'.

All the evidence goes to show that the civilians about the King were horrified at such a drastic proposal, and at the council meeting to discuss it the old Earl of Bristol[3] roundly declared that if Rupert got into the city he would probably set it on fire. The truth is that he and those who thought with him did not want a victory by force of arms—certainly not such a one as Rupert envisaged, for they were working and hoping for a peaceful settlement. Given the King's temperament, they had no great difficulty in carrying Charles along with them. He was so convinced of the righteousness of his cause that he kept hoping that before long his opponents would see reason if only he gave them a little time; so he delayed at Banbury, and then again at Oxford: he even allowed the sluggish Essex to march past him and get to London first, with the result that by the time he appeared before the capital it was too late.

The King's decision on this occasion was probably the most fatal of the war, and as the years went by and the royal cause declined, it must have riled Rupert to reflect that his advice had in all probability been right. By the summer of 1645 the fatal consequences of this decision had fully made themselves felt. The last Cavalier force fit to be called an army had been overwhelmed at Langport, while Bridgwater, on which great hopes had been placed, had been taken after a week's siege, and with it were lost magazines of food and ammunition which the Royalists could not hope to replace. It was in these circumstances that Rupert decided that the time had come for him to raise his voice again.

Up to this point the relations between uncle and nephew could not have been more cordial:

Nephew
    You will find so full a relation of the state of my affairs in
my Lord Digby's letter, that I will add nothing to that, but I
must observe to you that the chief hope of my resource is,
under God, from you, and I believe that if you had been with

[3] b. 1586, d. 1653.

me, I had not been put to those straits I am now in. I confess
the best had been to have followed your advice, yet if we had
rightly followed our own we had done well enough; but we too
easily quitted Abingdon, and were not so nimble upon their
loose quarters as we might have been, of which errors I must
acquit both myself and my Lord-General. It is here the loss
of Tewkesbury has put us to great inconvenience and hazards;
yet we doubt not but to defend ourselves until you may have
time to beat the Scots, but if you be too long in doing of it, I
apprehend some great inconvenience.

I will say no more at this time, but that I am

Your loving uncle, and most faithful friend
Charles R.

Worcester, 7th. June, 1644.

It is not until July of the following year that any serious difference of opinion can be detected between uncle and nephew.

Newport, 24 July 1645

Nephew

I having taken a resolution, wch is differing from what
I was most inclyned to, when I saw you last, I have thought
it most necessary to advertize you of it, albeit I cannot say
that the affirmative is so absolutely concluded on as the
negative; the particulars being of some length & greatest
service; I have commanded Digby to wryte it to you all in
Cypher, I not having tyme my selfe to doe it, & therefor
have chosen that part wch. I care not who reades, to witt,
my Affection to you and confidence in you. I needing no
other conjunction of service to you, than that if I knew you
not secrete, I would not at this time impart my resolution
to you.

I hereby thank you for the care you have taken in sending
over the Armes and Powder they being already come; as for
your two Regiments of Foot that I promised you, you shall
see that I doe not forget my word, wh. after to-morrow I
will make more plainly apeare, who am

Your loving Oncle and most faithfull friend
Charles R.

The resolution was presumably to go to Scotland, where Montrose was winning victory after victory. However this may be, the receipt of the King's letter prompted Rupert to write to the Duke of Richmond[4] from Bristol four days later:

> It is now in everybody's mouth that the King is going for Scotland. I must confesse it to be a strange resolution, considering not only in what condition he will leave all behind him, but what probability there is for him to go thither. If I am now desired to deliver my opinion; which your Lordship may declare to the King. His Majesty hath no way left to preserve his posterity, kingdom, and nobility, but by a treaty. I believe it is a more prudent way to retain something than to lose all.
>
> If the King resolves to abandon Ireland, which now he may with honour, since they desire unreasonably, and it is apparent they will cheat the King, having not 5,000 men in their power, when this has been told him, and that many of his officers and soldiers goe from him to them, if he have no more consideration of such as stay, and must extremely lament their condition; being exposed to all ruin and slavery. One comfort will be left; we shall all fall together, when this is, remember I have done my duty.

How much of a bombshell this letter really was to the King it is impossible to say, for he gave no immediate indication of his feelings, merely telling Richmond that 'dear Rupert' had been fully justified in writing so freely, but the difficulty lay not in consenting to a treaty but in asking for one—'it is a bitter draught the worse for having been previously tasted'.

Next day, when he had had time to give further thought to the matter, he answered Rupert at some length. He began by admitting that from his own standpoint his nephew was fully justified in giving the advice he did:

> for I confess that speaking as a mere soldier or statesman, I must say there is no probability but of my ruin; yet as a Christian I must tell you, that God will not suffer rebels and traitors to prosper, nor this cause to be overthrown.

[4] b. 1612, d. 1655. There are portraits of him at Kenwood; the Louvre; Metropolitan Museum, New York; Wilton House; and in the Duke of Buccleuch's collection.

He harboured no illusions about his own fate or prospects, for he goes on to say:

> Whatever personal punishment it shall please Him to inflict on me, must not make me repine, much less make me give over this quarrel; and there is as little question that a composition with them at this time is nothing else but a submission, which by the grace of God I am resolved against whatever it costs me; for I know my obligation to be both in conscience and honour, neither to abandon God's cause, injure my successors, nor forsake my friends.
>
> I cannot flatter myself with expectation of good success more than this, to end my days with honour and a good conscience, which obligeth me to continue my endeavours, in not despairing that God may yet in due time avenge his own cause.
>
> He that will stay with me at this time must expect and resolve either to die for a good cause or which is worse to live as miserable in maintaining it as the violence of insulting Rebels can make him.

Charles ended his letter by forbidding Rupert to mention a treaty to him again.

The scene now shifts to Bristol, which had been in Royalist hands since Rupert had captured it for the King in 1643, and of which he was still nominally governor. Its retention was of the utmost importance to the Royalist cause, for with Chester, which was already beleaguered by the Parliamentary forces, it was the only seaport of any size that still held out for the King, and if troops from Ireland were to arrive to turn the scale, it was through Bristol that they must come. Furthermore, as the fortunes of war were tending, Bristol might be expected to play a part not dissimilar to that of Tobruk in the Second World War on the flank of the enemy drive.

At first there would not appear to have been any realization of the fact that the place was in imminent danger, though the King seems to have felt that its garrison could do with some strengthening.

Ragland Fryday 11 July. 1645

Nephew

I hope that all the Foot with Sir Barnard Asheby will be
gone over by to-morrow at furthest & my two Troopes
before Wednesday next, wherefor I intend my selfe to pass on
Tewsday next at Blacke Roke, if you send me no other word,
howsoever, I desyre you to advertise me particularly (as
soone as you can) where I shall land, the night I passe over:
Charles Garat left me ether 4 or six peeces of Ordinance at
Cardife, which I have command to be carried to Bristol; I
intend them for the Feeld, but I leave them to you dispose as
you thinke best.

So I rest

Your loving Oncle & most faithful friend

Charles R.

Even a month later there seems to have been no disposition in
Bristol itself to view the situation tragically:

May it please your Highness

I take all the joy in the world in your good success—the
God of Heaven bless you. Sir Thomas Fairfax continues his
Siege at Sherborne, the new foot that came from London
came to him Monday night; they are in number seventeen
hundred. Here are seventeen old foot of your regiment come
from them: there are five hundred horse come to Bath from
Sherborne, they quartered last night at Phillips Norton: they
talk that they are going to assist the Scots.

Sir, this inclosed came for your Highness last night and
was open by the Governor of Gudhit Castle, that the bearer
was to say by word of mouth, was this, that they must be
speedily relieved for they want victuals; powder and bullet
they have enough but if they are not speedily relieved tis
lost; the Governor sends your Highness this word that three
thousand foot and two thousand horse would ruin their army.

The landings of the Irish is confirmed by several hands but
not so great a number, commanded by Colonel Fitzwilliam,
from London this news comes that Montrose is advanced into
England with fifteen thousand horse and foot, from the
West I hear nothing, when your Highness letters come from
Oxford I will speedily send them you.

Sir, I am very well pleased my little Captain Osborne did
so handsomely; and his hurt only a mark of honour, we are
settling the garrison according to your Highness orders; I
hear from gentlemen that come from Wales hitherways that
the King is still at Ludlow;
Sir, what intelligence I receive I shall present you with all
possible speed having as great inclination to serve you as any
person in the world being eternally obliged.

Your Highness
most obedient faithful
humble servant that honor you
with my heart and soul
H. Hawley

Bristol this
13th. August 1645

There was, however, now no Royalist army in the field to check
the Roundhead advance, but Rupert hurried to the city as soon as
he realized that it was threatened. The defences had been somewhat improved since he captured it two years before, but they
still left a good deal to be desired. Windmill Fort had been rebuilt
and rearmed, while Priors Hill Fort had also been strengthened,
but the curtain was still too low, and the ditch too wide and
shallow. With a garrison of only 1,500 men, Rupert was called
upon to hold a perimeter of four miles against the New Model
Army of several times his strength, while at his back was a city
stricken with the plague, and of which the inhabitants were
hostile to the royal cause owing to the ruthless manner in which
they had been taxed during the occupation by the King's
troops.

By the end of August, Fairfax had completed the investment of
the place, and on 4 September he summoned Rupert to surrender
in terms in which the *argumentum ad hominem* played an important part, for after referring to the efforts made by Englishmen
in the Palatinate cause in earlier years he went on:

Let all England judge, whether the burning of its towns,
ruining of its cities, and destroying of its people, be a good
requital from a person of your family, which had the prayers,
tears, and blood of its Parliament and people.

What impression this appeal made upon Rupert we have no means of knowing, but he refused the demand to surrender.

Fairfax, whose superiority in artillery had enabled him to make a practicable breach, replied by ordering a general assault. On the south and south-east his storming parties were repulsed with heavy losses, but on the west he made several lodgments within the curtain walls: the forts proved more difficult, and Priors Hill in particular held out for hours, but at last the Roundheads broke in, and put its defenders to the sword, as was increasingly becoming the habit of the New Model when victorious. Rupert's men fell back through the streets, where they received little support from the populace, but what really made his position hopeless was the fact that the enemy infantry had infiltrated between the castle and the forts that still held out.

In these difficult circumstances Rupert opened negotiations for surrender, but intimated that the terms would have to be approved by the King: this condition was rejected by Fairfax, who probably suspected in them an excuse to delay matters until Royalist reinforcements would have time to arrive. Accordingly Rupert, with the approval of a council of war, accepted the terms offered by the Roundhead commander, and very generous they were, for not only was the garrison allowed to march out with all the honours of war, but they were even supplied with muskets and ammunition against enemy attacks on their march to Oxford.

The hand-over, which took place on 12 September must have been a dramatic and pathetic scene. First of all came detachments of the Royalist horse and foot, then baggage-waggons; next more infantry and, following them, Rupert's red-coated life-guards dismounted, carrying at the ready the muskets with which Fairfax had supplied them. After them came Rupert himself, resplendent in scarlet 'very richly laid in silver lace', and mounted on a black Barbary horse, with behind him mounted life-guards, and a number of senior officers of both sides apparently riding amicably together. Fairfax throughout treated Rupert with the utmost courtesy, and there was much sweeping of hats when he and Cromwell finally parted from the defeated Prince. We are, however, told by a Parliamentary chronicler that as the Royalist cavalry passed through the gates the Ironsides of the New Model could not refrain from laughter at the miserable appearance of their once formidable opponents with their sorry nags, their wretched equipment, and their downcast looks.

It is not difficult to understand why Fairfax granted such easy terms. He knew that the fate of Bristol was sealed, but he wanted to capture it as a city and not as a mass of smouldering ruins, for he was under no illusions but that Rupert would put fire to the place if driven to extremes; nor did it matter if the garrison was allowed to proceed to the Royalist headquarters at Oxford: the war was over anyhow, and nothing now remained to be done except a certain amount of mopping up. Fairfax was thus justified on every score in the line he took, but how about Rupert? Did he do the right thing, or were the King's strictures merited.

From the day that Rupert surrendered Bristol until the present time this question has been argued, though modern military historians have been inclined to hold that he had no other course open to him than the one he adopted. His position was hopeless, and although he might have held out for a few days longer, it was only a question of time before he would have been forced to surrender, having in the interval sustained serious losses. As it was, he had safely brought off some 800 horse and 1,000 foot, who might otherwise have been massacred like the defenders of Priors Hill. This was reason enough to the professional soldier, who deemed that the moment when he found himself faced by inevitable defeat was the best moment to hoist the white flag—the King who saw the war as a crusade took a very different view.

His immediate reaction was to write the following letter to Rupert:

Hereford, 14 Sept. 1645

Nephew

Though the loss of Bristol be a great blow to me, yet your surrendering it as you did, is of so much affliction to me, that it makes me not only forget the considerations of that place, but is likewise the greatest trial of my constancy that hath yet befallen me; for what is to be done, after one that is so near me as you are, both in blood and friendship, submits himself to so mean an action? (I give it the easiest term) such—I have so much to say, that I will say no more of it: only, lest rashness of judgment be laid to my charge, I must remember you of your letter of the 12th. of August,

whereby you assured me, that, if no mutiny happened, you
would keep Bristol for four months. Did you keep it four
days? Was there any thing like a mutiny?

More questions might be asked, but now, I confess, to
little purpose: my conclusion is, to desire you to seek your
subsistence, until it shall please God to determine of my condition, somewhere beyond seas; to which end I send you a
pass; and I pray God to make you sensible of your present
condition, and give you means to redeem what you have
lost; for I shall have no greater joy in a victory than a just
occasion without blushing to assure you of my being

> Your loving uncle, and most faithful friend.
> Charles R.

The pass ran as follows:

Charles R.

Charles by the Grace of God, King of England, Scotland,
France, and Ireland, Defender of the Faith etc. To Admirals,
Vice-Admirals, Governors, and Captains of Ports, Ships, and
Forts, Mayors, Sheriffs, Justices of the Peace . . . and loving
subjects whom it may concern, Greeting.

Whereas we have granted . . . a Licence unto our Nephew
Prince Rupert to pass from these Dominions into the parts
beyond the seas; these are therefore to will and command
every of you, not only to permit him with all his servants,
horses, and all his necessaries to pass by you and embark at
any of the Ports within my Dominions, and from thence to
transport himself accordingly; but likewise to afford him all
assistance and fitting accommodation in his said journey,
whereof you are not to fail: And for so doing this shall be
your warrant.

> Given at our Court at (Undated)
> By his Majesty's Command
> George Digby

Further evidence of the King's reaction to what must have been
the greatest shock he had sustained since the murder of Buckingham may be found in the letter which he wrote to Rupert's
brother, Prince Maurice:[5]

[5] b. 1620, d. (drowned at sea) 1654.

Newton, September 20, 1645

Nephew

What through want of time, or unwillingness to speak to you of so unpleasing a subject, I have not yet (which I now must supply) spoken to you freely of your brother Rupert's present condition. The truth is, that his unhandsome quitting the castle and fort of Bristol hath enforced me to put him off those commands in my army, and have sent him a pass to go beyond seas; now, though I could do no less than this, for which, believe me, I have too much reason upon strict examination, yet I assure you that I am most confident that this great error of his (which, indeed, hath given me more grief than any misfortune since this damnable rebellion) hath no ways proceeded from his change of affection to me or my cause; but merely by having his judgement seduced by rotten-hearted villains making fair pretensions to him; and I am resolved so little to forget his former services that, whensoever it shall please God to enable me to look upon my friends like a king, he shall thank God for the pains he hath spent in my armies. So much for him. Now for yourself. I know you to be so free from his present misfortune that it no way staggers me in that good opinion which I have ever had of you; and, so long as you shall not weary of your employments under me, I will give you all the encouragement and contentment that lies in my power; however, you shall always find me

Your loving uncle, and most assured friend,

Charles R.

Rupert, however, was not the only victim of the King's wrath, for Charles gave some drastic instructions to Sir Edward Nicholas:[6]

Hereford, September 14, 1645

Nicholas

When you shall have considered the strange and most inexcusable delivering up of the castle and fort of Bristol, and compared it with those many preceding advertisements which have been given me, I make no doubt but you and all my Council there will conclude that I could do no less than

[6] Secretary of State.

what you find here enclosed, in my case for the preservation of my son, of all you faithful servants there, and of that important place, my city of Oxford.

In the first place, you will find a copy of my letter to my nephew; secondly, a revocation of his commission of general; thirdly, a warrant to Lieutenant-Colonel Hamilton to exercise the charge of lieutenant-governor of Oxford in Sir Thomas Glenham's absence; fourthly, a warrant to the said Lieutenant-Colonel Hamilton to apprehend the person of Will Legge, present governor of Oxford; and lastly, a warrant to be directed to whatever person shall be thought fittest for the apprehending my nephew Rupert, in case of such extremity as shall be hereafter specified, but not otherwise.

As for the circumstances and the timing of the execution of all these particulars, as far forth as they may admit of some hours' delay more or less, I must refer it to my Lord Treasurer's care and yours to advise of, upon the place, how it may be done with the most security and accordingly to direct the manner of proceeding. But yet I tell you my opinion as far forth as I can judge at this distance, which is, that you should begin with securing the person of Will Legge, before anything be declared concerning my nephew. But that once done, then the sooner you declare to the Lords the revoking of my nephew's commission, and my making Sir Thomas Glenham[7] governor of Oxford, the better. As for the delivering of my letter to my nephew, if he be at Oxford, I take the proper time for that to be as soon as possibly may be after the securing of Will Legge. But if my nephew be not there, I would then have you hasten my letter unto him; and in the meantime, put the rest in execution.

Lastly, I enjoin you to let all the Lords know, that whatever is done in this kind is out of my tender regard for their safety and preservation; and they shall speedily receive for their satisfaction a particular account of the reasons for this necessary proceeding. I rest

Your most assured friend
Charles R.

Tell my son that I shall less grieve to hear that he is knocked on the head than he should do so mean an action

[7] A Royalist general.

as is the rendering of Bristol castle and fort upon the terms it was.

C. R.

These three letters fully explain the King's attitude, though whether he had already become suspicious as a result of Rupert's earlier suggestion that he should come to terms with the Parliament, and consequently was prepared to take a jaundiced view of all he said or did, cannot be established in default of the relevant evidence. What cannot be questioned is that there were several members of the royal entourage who were violently prejudiced against Rupert, and who lost no opportunity to put the worst possible construction on his deeds and words. Foremost among them was Digby, who had been working night and day against the Prince, while outwardly professing undying friendship. Naseby had already played into his hands, and he had written a long letter to their mutual friend, Will Legge, in which by inference he saddled Rupert with the whole blame for the defeat. An extract from Legge's reply is sufficient to explain the subsequent enmity of the two men, and to render it more than likely that Digby was behind the King's order to put Legge under arrest:

> I am extremely afflicted to understand from you that Prince Rupert and yourself should be upon so unkindly terms, and I protest I have cordially endeavoured, with all my interest in his Highness, to incline him to a friendship with your Lordship, conceiving it a matter of advantage to my master's service to have a good intelligence between persons so eminently employed in his affairs, and likewise the great obligation and inclination I had to either of you. But truly, my Lord, I often found this a hard matter to hold between you; and your last letter gives me cause to think that your Lordship is not altogether free from what he accused you of as the reason of his jealousies. Which was that you both say and do things to his prejudice, contrary to your confessions, and not in an open and direct line, but obscurely and obliquely; and this under your Lordship's pardon, I find your letter very full of.

As for the accusation that Rupert was meditating, presumably with the troops from Bristol, a *coup d'état* at Oxford, can only

18

have originated in the malicious imaginations of Digby and his associates. In all the circumstances Charles's reaction was understandable; to some extent not unnatural; but certainly unfortunate.

Now to return to Rupert. Immediately after the fall of Bristol he wrote to the King in justification of what he had done, and asked for an audience. The letter is admittedly somewhat verbose, and not really calculated to appease Charles, but considering the mood in which his uncle was, it would have been difficult to have appeased him anyhow:

Sir

I have received both your letters of the same tenor, from Ragland, September 14th., with other intimations of your pleasure of the same date, which, as far as my power can make them, are already obeyed: my not having any command, or meddling in your service, rendering it very easy for me to comply with your will to have it so; for no other motive or consideration first or last made me an actor but to do you service, and that as you desired. How I have behaved myself, from the beginning until the misfortune of your commands engaged me in Bristol, from inferior persons I shall not desire greater justification or applause than that which I have received from your Majesty, therefore I pass all former times without mention, and come to this; of which I only say, that if your Majesty had vouchsafed me so much patience as to hear me inform you, before you had made a final judgement—I will presume to present this much—that you would not have censured me as it seems you do: and that I should have given you as just satisfaction as in any former occasion, though not so happy. But since there is so great appearance that I must suffer, that it is already decreed; what otherwise I should have desired to have given your Majesty an account, now I am obliged to seek for my own clearing: that, what you will have me bear, may be with as much honour to me as belongs to integrity. If your Majesty will admit me to that opportunity, I desire to wait on you to that end as soon as I can, when I know I have your leave for it, which I humbly desire to have.

If I must be so unfortunate not to be allowed (if, since the first duty that I owe which is to your Majesty, is not suffered me, to perform wherein else I should rest) in the next place I owe myself that justice as to publish to the world what I think will clear my erring, in all this business now in question, from any foul deed or neglect, and vindicate me from your desert of any prevailing malice, though I suffer it. Your commands that I should dispose of myself somewhere beyond seas, be pleased to consider of whether it be in my power (though you have sent me a pass), as times now are, to go by it. Wherever I am, or how unhappy soever, and of your will made so, yet I shall ever retain that duty to your Majesty which I ever, as

Your Majesty's most humble, and most obedient

Nephew, and faithful humble servant

Rupert

Sept. 1645

The request for an audience was understandable, for the two men had not met since 22 July, five weeks after Naseby, when they had done so at Blackrock, and Rupert had shown himself somewhat less than enthusiastic about a scheme of the King's to cross the Severn and help Goring,[8] who had just been defeated at Langport. The suggestion that there might now be a meeting between uncle and nephew horrified Digby and his friends, more particularly as the King wished to go to Worcester where Maurice was governor: at all costs he must be removed from influences favourable to Rupert or he would learn the baseness of their accusations against him, so they persuaded him to go to Newark, where he received his nephew's letter.

So he was not in Oxford when Rupert arrived there on 16 September, to find that everybody was on his side. There he remained waiting for an answer from his uncle which never came, so he determined to see the King whether the monarch liked it or not. On 8 October he left Oxford with about a hundred mounted Cavaliers, and at Banbury he was joined by his brother, Maurice, with a score or so more. Part of the journey was through a countryside under enemy occupation, but in several brushes with Parliamentary troops Rupert was victorious, and the brothers duly arrived at Belvoir. When he heard that they were on their way,

[8] b. 1608, d. 1657.

Digby announced that he would take the field to assist the Scottish Royalists, and very wisely left for the north.

The King had not the least desire to see Rupert, and is said to have declared that in his present mood his nephew was 'no fit company for him'; anyhow he wrote requiring 'him to stay at Belvoir till further order', and reprehending him 'for not having given obedience to his former commands'; but the Prince was not to be deterred, and the next night when Charles was waiting for his supper to be announced, Rupert and Maurice walked into the room. The former briefly stated that he had come to defend himself in the matter of the surrender of Bristol, but the King took little notice of him, though he allowed both brothers to stand by his chair while he ate: he addressed a few remarks to Maurice, but none to Rupert, and as soon as the meal was over he went to bed. By the following morning he had second thoughts, and granted his nephew a court-martial, which was very fairly composed of friends and enemies, before which Rupert gave an account of the Bristol operations, and stated his case generally. There were two sittings, at the second of which Charles presided in person, and the result was a unanimous verdict, signed by the King, declaring that 'Our said right dear nephew is not guilty of any the least want of courage or fidelity to us or our service in that action'. There the matter should have ended, and that it did not was almost entirely due to Rupert: indeed, whatever sympathy one may have with him over the way he was treated by his uncle after the surrender of Bristol, it is difficult to have any over his behaviour in this later incident.

It happened that the Governor of Newark was one Sir Richard Willis, who was a staunch friend of Rupert, and had called attention to the fact by riding out to meet him with an escort of cavalry. At this unfortunate juncture it was announced that Willis was to command the King's Life Guards, and that Lord Bellasys, a supporter of Digby, was to replace him as Governor of Newark. Now in a sense this was promotion for Willis, but it meant leaving Newark, and he took his new appointment badly, as did Rupert and his other friends. So one Sunday evening when the King was just sitting down to dinner—Rupert seems to have had an unfortunate habit of intruding upon his uncle at mealtimes—the two Princes, Sir Richard Willis, Lord Gerard,[9] and about twenty

[9] Charles, Colonel, later General (Baron 1645), d. 1667.

21

officers walked into the room. Willis at once began to proclaim his wrongs, and to demand satisfaction. Whereupon Charles rose from the table, had his dinner taken away, and ordered all the junior officers to leave the room.

He then stepped over to a table in the window, and beckoned to the leading malcontents to follow him, whereupon there ensued what by any standards can only be described as a disgraceful scene. Willis commenced proceedings by voicing his complaints, and while he was speaking Rupert interrupted to say that Willis was to be removed from his governorship for no fault he had committed, but for being his friend, and Gerard interjected that it was the plot of Digby, who was a traitor, as he would prove him to be. What followed is best told in Clarendon's words:

> The King was so surprised with this manner of behaviour, that he rose in some disorder, and would have gone into his bedchamber; calling Sir Richard Willis to follow him; who answered aloud, 'that he had received a public injury, and therefore that he expected a public satisfaction.' This, with what had passed (before). so provoked His Majesty, that, with greater indignation than he was ever seen possessed with, he commanded them 'to depart from his presence, and to come no more into it'; and this with such circumstances in his looks and gesture, as well as words that they appeared no less confounded; and departed the room, ashamed of what they had done; and yet as soon as they came to the Governor's house, they sounded to horse, intending to be presently gone.

The next act in this remarkable drama was the receipt by the King, that same day according to Clarendon, of a document signed by Rupert, Maurice, and about twenty-four officers, in which they desired that

> Sir Richard Willis might receive a trial by a court of war; and if they found him faulty, then to be dismissed from his charge: and that if this might not be granted, they desired passes for themselves, and as many as desired to go with them.

At the same time they hoped that His Majesty would not look

upon this action of theirs as a mutiny. To this last request Charles somewhat drily replied that he 'would not now christen it, but it looked very like one', while 'as for the court of war, he would not make that a judge of his actions; but for the passes, they should be immediately prepared for as many as desired to have them'. The next morning the passes were sent to them, and to the number of about two hundred they left Newark.

Rupert, however, showed no immediate inclination to take advantage of his pass, whereupon the King issued a further statement to the effect that, although he had granted passes to him and his brother, 'His Majesty did not intend that they should reside any long time in any garrison to the destruction of provisions or the debauchery of our officers and soldiers, and therefore begs them to proceed on their journey or they will be considered as having violated the passes'.

Rupert was still at Belvoir when this communication reached him, and it was from there, on 31 October, that he replied:

Sir
    Your Majesty's of the thirtieth of the present I received this Friday. I wonder at the argument of it, that your Majesty should conclude I intended the destruction of your garrisons by wasting their provisions; I should find out a more prejudicial way of disserving you if I had any such intention. As for the debauching of any of your Majesty's officers and soldiers . . . I never spoke to any of them, nor has any officer to my knowledge animadverted any such thing. As for my stay in your quarters 'tis but till I have a pass from the Parliament to go beyond the seas which I expect hourly, and then I hope I shall quit your Majesty of further trouble concerning our stay in your quarters, though I did not expect to be proceeded against as a person out of your Majesty's protection, if I had made my stay longer than I intend. Sir, give me leave to tell you . . . at my departure, the meanest subject you have could not be so unkind and unnaturally treated with, however it shall never lessen my respects to your Majesty. . . .
                    Your Majesty's Most Obedient Nephew
                            and faithful servant
                                Rupert

Meanwhile there were powerful forces working for a reconciliation between uncle and nephew, and foremost among them was Colonel William Legge, whom the King had now released from imprisonment, and who is found writing to Rupert under date of 21 November:

My most dear Prince

The liberty that I have got is but of little contentment when divided from you. Four days after his Majesty's arrival here Mr. Ashburnham[10] fetched me to kiss his hand, without any expostulation for my commitment, since which I have waited in the chamber. The first discourse I had with him was concerning you, where he gave me a relation of the unhappy breach between you, which I would to God had never been. But now that what is past cannot be recalled, I should humbly beseech you to look forward to what may be the best for your future honour and advantage. Since I had the honour to be your servant I never had other desire than faithfully to serve you, and when I leave to pursue that, may I die forgotten!

I have not hitherto lost a day without moving his Majesty to recal you, and truly this very day he protested to me he would count it a great happiness to have you with him, so he received that satisfaction he is bound in honour to have, and that that is, you will receive from the Duke of Richmond. The King says, as he is your uncle, he is in the nature of a parent to you, and swears that if Prince Charles had done as you did he would never see him without the same he desires from you: I beseech you consider well of your affairs, and let me but receive your directions, and there never shall be anything wanting that may render me,

Your most obliged faithful servant
W. Legge

By the time Rupert had received his Parliamentary passports from London, and he could have gone abroad whenever he wished, but such letters as these deterred him, for in addition to Legge there was Lord Dorset[11] writing, 'If my prayers can

[10] b. 1603, d. 1671.
[11] b. 1590, d. 1651.

prevail, you shall not have the heart to leave us all in our saddest times . . . resolve, princely Sir, to sink or swim with the King.' Charles, of course, was demanding an apology for the scene at Newark, but so softened was Rupert by the appeals he was receiving that when Charles sent him the draft of a carefully worded apology for his signature he tore it up and returned a blank paper with his name at the bottom, thus indicating that his uncle might have any form of apology he desired. We are told that when the King saw it tears came into his eyes.

The two men met in Oxford and their reconciliation was complete, though Rupert would not appear to have been restored to any military command: this, however, was of no great significance, for the war was nearly finished. That the old confidence between uncle and nephew had been restored was proved by the King's disclosure to the latter that he proposed to surrender to the Scots; Rupert argued strongly against any such step, but when he found that Charles was obdurate, characteristically offered to accompany him. The offer was, however, refused, for the King pointed out that he and his party were to travel in disguise, and his nephew's great height would betray them.

So when Charles rode out of Oxford on 27 April 1646, Rupert and Maurice remained in the doomed city, and there they stayed until its capture by Fairfax in the following June, when, after some bickering with the Parliament about the renewal of their passes, they were allowed to proceed overseas.

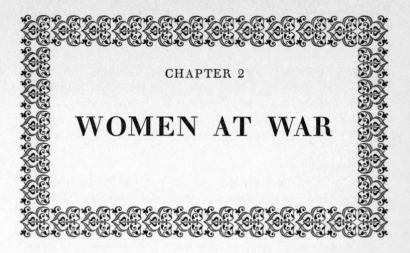

CHAPTER 2

WOMEN AT WAR

1 The Countess of Derby

For a variety of reasons women played a more prominent part on the Royalist than on the Roundhead side: probably the outstanding one was that their husbands were away fighting for the King and they were left to hold the family seat, be it a castle or a large country-house. An outstanding example of this was the wife of the seventh Earl of Derby. She was born Charlotte de la Tremouille, the daughter of Claude, Duc de Thouars, by Charlotte Brabantine, daughter of William of Orange, and she is said to have brought him a marriage portion of £24,000.

The Countess was an important factor in the King's calculations. On the strategic side Lathom House in Lancashire, where she lived, had considerable value, as had the Isle of Man, which was a Stanley possession, the Earl of Derby being King of Man. Then. Then, her relationship with the House of Orange was of the greatest value, for the political situation in the Netherlands was not only very confused but was of great concern to Charles. There was, as we shall see, a pull-devil, pull-baker struggle in progress for control of the country between the burghers of Amsterdam,

27

who in foreign affairs backed the Parliament, and the Princes of Orange who were favourable to the King. The ruling Stadtholder was Frederick Henry, and until his death in 1647 he was instrumental in supplying Charles with money and munitions. So the closer the links with the House of Orange the better, and one of them was undoubtedly the Countess of Derby. It was probably with a view to keeping in his good graces that she wrote the following somewhat nebulous letter[1] to Frederick Henry:

Monseigneur

Nothing on earth can give me greater satisfaction than to know that Your Highness is in good health and that you do me the honour of remembering your great-neice. I shall never forget that happy moment. We are here in a miserable and God-forsaken state, and the King has great need of all his friends and servants, among whom Your Highness is the foremost. I am sure that with your usual generosity you will give him the assistance he needs.

My husband is with him to report on what he has done. I wish that all the nobles were as devoted to him, and had the same strength and will to serve him as he has. His Majesty should soon, from what he says, be here where I believe his presence is very necessary.

I am writing to M. Nuges about a matter of importance to me but on which I do not venture to trouble Your Highness except to say that the revenues, that my late mother had, have never been paid in compensation for the trouble and work which your father, of glorious memory, took for the benefit of bastards and persons whose parentage and date of birth are unknown, and who do not know the name of their father.

I hope that Your Highness will remember that I had the honour to be married in your house, with your permission; and that you will do my children and me the honour of protecting our due rights: which is the humble prayer to Your Highness of your most humble, obedient and faithful great-niece and servant,

Charlotte de la Tremouille

Lathom, 15 August, 1642

[1] The original is in French.

In those early days it was generally assumed that, to quote
Clarendon, so far as Lancashire and Cheshire were concerned,
Lord Derby had 'a greater influence upon these two counties, and
a more absolute command over the people in them, than any
subject in England had in any other quarter of the kingdom'.
Unhappily for the King the war had not long been in progress
before this proved not to be the case, and so the original Royalist
plan of campaign in this area, which was that the Royalists of
Lancashire should bolster up those of Cheshire, had to be
abandoned, for Lord Derby

> found Lancashire to be almost possessed against him; the
> rebels every day gaining and fortifying all the strong towns,
> and surprising his troops, without any considerable encounter.
> And yet, so hard was the King's condition, that, though he
> knew those great misfortunes proceeded from want of
> conduct, and of a vigorous and expert commander, he
> thought it not safe to make any alteration, lest that Earl
> might be provoked, out of disdain to have any superior in
> Lancashire, to manifest how much he could do against him,
> though it appeared he could do little for him. Yet it was
> easily discerned, that his ancient power there depended more
> upon the fear than love of the people; there being very
> many, now in this time of liberty, engaging themselves
> against the King, that they might not be subject to that
> lord's commands.

In effect, from the King's point of view, the seventh Earl of
Derby was in many ways more of a liability than an asset.

In these circumstances, as the war progressed, the Parliamentarians turned their attention to what was then Lord Derby's
principal Lancashire seat, namely Lathom House. In compliance
with a resolution taken in the Parliamentary Council at Manchester on Saturday, 24 February 1644, a force under Sir Thomas
Fairfax appeared before Lathom House, and summoned the
Countess of Derby and her garrison of three hundred to surrender:

> To My Lady Derby to surrender the Garrison of Lathom
>   Being sent hither over this part by command from the
> Parliament to suppress and prevent all force that shall

oppose their legal just power, and to prevent the increasing miseries of some almost reunited counties, which, by God's great goodness, hath had some happy success; and understanding that your Ladyship keeps Lathom with a garrison of soldiers in it, which doth many injuries to the army and much hinders them, and is a receptacle and great encouragement to the Papists and disaffected persons in those parts, (which I cannot believe your Ladyship doth naturally affect); I should not do my duty if I neglect the means to remove that mischief, Yet, Madam, I do owe you that so much honour as a lady, as I would use all just means that would make me capable of serving your Ladyship, and proceed so as may testify so much, though some force be already near your Ladyship.

I desire to have sent your Ladyship herein inclosed an Act of Parliament (indeed I have need to excuse it to your Ladyship I had not a better to send you, having passed many hands, there being but this in the county) that your Ladyship, may make use of the clemency of Parliament. And if the Earl of Derby will make an advantage of it I shall faithfully serve his Lordship in it, and if your Ladyship so render up that place, Lathom House, I shall offer such terms as may be honourable and convenient for your Ladyship, not but the Parliament, which aims at nothing but the establishment of true religion, and the honour and peace of the King and kingdom, will have a tender respect and care over your Ladyship.

I will add no more, but an assurance to your Ladyship only I say this to prevent such that may happen, and to do your Ladyship the best service that is in the power of

Your Ladyship's most faithful and humble servant
Thos. Fairfax

To these overtures Lady Derby answered that

she much wondered that Sir Thomas Fairfax should require her to give up her lord's house, without any offence on her part done to the Parliament; desiring in a business of such weight, that struck both at her religion and life, that so nearly concerned her sovereign, her lord, and her whole

posterity, she might have a week's consideration, both to
resolve the doubts of conscience and to advise in matters
of law and honour.

What Lady Derby was playing for was, of course, time in the
hope that she would be relieved, but this was precisely what
Fairfax was determined not to give her; so he replied that he
could not grant her request, but suggested that she should come
out in his coach, and discuss the position with him and the
leading Parliamentary officers. Needless to say the Countess at
once saw the trap, and answered that 'notwithstanding her present
condition, she remembered her lord's honour and her own birth,
and conceived it more likely that Sir Thomas Fairfax should wait
upon her than she upon him'. Other conditions were afterwards
proposed, but she rejected them all as dishonourable or uncertain.

At this point, and probably still in the hope of gaining time,
Lady Derby in her turn proposed conditions which were to the
effect that she should continue for a month in Lathom House, and
that she should then, with her children, friends, soldiers, and
servants depart and have free transport to the Isle of Man, while
after her departure no soldier should be quartered in the lordship
of Lathom nor any garrison put into Lathom or Knowsley House,
and that none of her tenants, neighbours, or friends then in the
House with her should for assisting her suffer in their persons or
estates. By this time, however, Fairfax's patience was exhausted,
and he demanded that Lathom House should be evacuated by ten
o'clock the following morning.

The reply he received from Lady Derby was to the effect that

she refused this offer, and was truly happy that hers had
been refused, protesting that she would rather hazard her
life than offer the like again; and that, though a woman and
a stranger, divorced from her friends and robbed of her
estate, she was ready to receive their utmost violence,
trusting in God both for protection and deliverance.

After some further unsuccessful negotiations the siege commenced. Lathom House was well suited for defence; it stood upon
flat ground, and at the time of the siege was surrounded by a
strong wall some six feet thick. On the wall were nine towers
flanking each other, and in every tower were six cannon which

played three one way and three the other. Within the wall was a moat, eight yards wide and two yards deep, while upon the edge of the moat, between the wall and the ditch, was a row of palisades: in the middle of the building itself there was the Eagle Tower which surmounted all the others. On the towers the Countess placed snipers with instructions to pick off the Roundhead officers whenever they made their appearance. The works of the besiegers, it may be added, formed a line of circumvallation drawn round the house at a distance of between sixty and two hundred yards from the wall as best suited the ground.

As might have been expected under the command of so spirited a woman as Lady Derby, the garrison was not slow in taking the initiative, and on 10 March they made a sally upon the works of the besiegers. They were led by a Captain Farmer, and the foray would appear to have been remarkably successful, for the Parliamentarians lost thirty men killed and six taken prisoner. For the next ten days there was sporadic fighting of minor importance, but on the 20th the besiegers brought one of their cannon into action against the pinnacles and turrets of the house. On the same day the fighting was interrupted when Fairfax produced a letter which he had received from the Earl of Derby, who was at Chester in which he asked for an honourable and free passage for his wife, if she desired it, and children, as he was unwilling to expose them to the hazards of a siege: the Countess, however, would have none of this, but replied that 'she would willingly submit herself to her lord's commands; but till she was assured it was his pleasure by correspondence she would neither yield the house nor desert it, but wait for the event, according to the will of God'.

The beginning of April was marked by considerable activity on the part of the Roundhead artillery, but it appears to have been more of a nuisance than a menace: at any rate the besiegers invoked heavenly aid, for they besought any minister of religion and well-wishers in the county to offer up their prayers for the fall of Lathom House. More effective appears to have been another sortie under the leadership of Captain Farmer, who, at the head of 140 men, issued out of a postern-gate, beat the enemy back from the works they had erected round the house, spiked all their guns, and killed about fifty men; the operation, it may be added, was supervised by a Captain Fox from the Eagle Tower who directed it by means of flags.

By this time Fairfax had gone North to join the Scots and besiege York, and the command of the parliamentary forces devolved
on a local Roundhead lawyer called Rigby. On 25 April he sent
what he called his last message to Lady Derby calling on her to
surrender Lathom House with everybody and everything in it
into his hands, and to receive the mercy of the Parliament. Having
read this summons Lady Derby had the messenger who had
brought it paraded before her, when she told him that 'a due
reward for his pains would be to be hanged up at the gates', but
'thou art only a foolish instrument of a traitor's pride': whereupon
she tore up the summons to surrender, and continued:

> Tell that insolent rebel he shall neither have persons, goods,
> nor house. When our strength and provisions are spent
> we shall find a fire more merciful than Rigby; and then, if
> the providence of God prevent it not, my goods and house
> shall burn in his sight; and myself, children, and soldiers,
> rather than fall into his hands, will seal our religion and loyalty
> in the same flame.

We are told that these words were uttered in front of the
garrison, and were greeted with tumultuous applause.

Alternate fighting and negotiating occupied most of May, and
on the 23rd of that month a further summons to surrender came
from Rigby, and it contained an offer of mercy, but to this Lady
Derby replied that 'the mercies of the wicked are cruel', and that
unless they treated with her husband 'they should never take her
or any of her friends alive', Meanwhile, however, events were
taking place elsewhere which were to bring the siege to an end.

On 25 April Rupert had come to Oxford to discuss the summer
campaign with the King: he had already appealed to Ireland
for assistance to be sent to Lord Derby:

> May it please your Highness
> According and in obedience to your command in your letter
> of the 5th of this month, and in pursuance of like commands
> sent me from his Majesty by Colonel Trafford, I am now
> preparing three companies, well armed and commanded, to
> be sent into North Wales where, God willing, they will be
> by the end of next week, or very soon after, to receive your
> Highness's pleasure.

In things within my power your Highness's pleasure shall no sooner be understood than obeyed by me, and I trust my performances shall at least correspond with my undertakings; but in things depending upon the abilities or inclinations of others, though I shall very rarely be positive in them, yet I may sometimes be mistaken in the promises of others, when I see probability for it. Of this nature were your Highness's commands touching the procuring of arms and ammunition from His Majesty's Roman Catholic subjects of this Kingdom whereof, though I remember I gave your Highness no full assurance, yet I confess I was, when I wrote, in greater hope of providing them than now I am.

Nor are they very much to be blamed, the Scots being yet here[2] in very great numbers, and fresh reports coming daily that they will not only begin the war afresh with them, but endeavour to impose the taking of the Covenant upon us by force of arms. Yet if your Highness shall command shipping and provision hither, I shall be able to send eight hundred or one thousand good men reasonably well armed. But without shipping and provisions be sent, our wants are such that I shall be able to do little towards recruiting the army under your Highness's command. I most humbly beseech your Highness's pardon for the plainness of this letter and the trouble it gives you, and to be pleased to dispose entirely of

Your Highness's most faithful, humble, and obedient

Ormond[3]

His Majesty's Castle of Dublin
18th. April, 1644

I most humbly and earnestly beseech your Highness to make use of your power towards the release of those gallant men that were sent hence and are now prisoners; your Highness's favours to me give me boldness to let you know I cannot be more obliged in the person of any man than in that of Colonel Henry Warren.

Eleven days later Rupert received another letter from Dublin:

[2] They had arrived in the spring of 1642.
[3] b. 1610, d. 1688. Twelfth Earl and subsequently first Duke. Lord Lieutenant of Ireland on several occasions under Charles I and Charles II. A strong Protestant and close friend of Hyde.

May it please your Highness

Now that Captain John Bartlets is arrived I hope within
a few days to send over three hundred good men and well
armed, God send them a safe passage for I hear the
Parliament ships are upon that Coast.

Your Highness before now I doubt not is informed that
there is little hopes for the present to be supplied hence with
any considerable proportion of Arms or ammunition, but
if I had means to keep them together, and send them over,
I should be able to send good bodies of men.

I received his Majestie's command to furnish my Lord of
Derby with six iron pieces, but being ignorant what use your
Highness may have of such for the defence of North Wales
which if it should be lost would cut off all hope of assistance
to his Majesty from hence I intend to send these pieces
which is all I can spare with Bartlet to be there disposed of
or sent to the Isle of Man as your Highness shall think fit.

There is one Lloyd and Bradshaw that desire to have
letters of marque from me, but the persons being unknown
to me I humbly refer them to your Highness and rest

Your Highness most humble faithful

and obedient servant

Ormonde

Dublin Castle, 29 April 1644

As a result of the deliberations between the King and Rupert
it was decided that the first step in the summer campaign should
be to relieve York; so on 16 May the Prince marched out of
Shrewsbury at the head of 2,000 horse and 6,000 foot, and on the
25th he took Stockport. When the news of this reached Rigby he
decided that it was time for him to be off, so he raised the siege,
and fell back on Bolton, which was Roundhead to a man.

The first Royalist assault on that town was repulsed with loss,
and the elated Parliamentarians made the mistake of hanging
one of their Irish prisoners from the walls. Now there was
nothing that annoyed Rupert more than the assumption that the
Irish were beyond the rules of civilized war, and when he captured Bolton at the next assault he made the defenders pay dearly
for their barbarity, or, as Defoe puts it in his ingenious historical
reconstruction entitled the *Memoirs of a Cavalier*, 'our men got

some plunder here, which the Parliament made a great noise about; but it was their due, and they bought it dear enough.' With Rupert was Lord Derby, who had private wrongs of his own and his wife's to avenge, and almost the first person he met on entering the town was a former servant of his who had deserted from Lathom House and directed the besiegers' artillery with considerable skill. The Earl ran him through without the least compunction, but it is to be feared that there was less excuse for the numerous other killings which took place. A pleasanter feature of the affair was Rupert's visit to Lathom House, when he formally thanked Lady Derby for her services to the King and handed over to her the flags of Rigby's beaten army.

After the raising of the siege Lord and Lady Derby retired to the Isle of Man, and the care of Lathom House was handed over to Colonel Rawstorne, who before long was himself besieged there by the Parliamentarians: by this time, however, the war had turned against the Royalists, Rupert had been defeated at Marston Moor, and there was no chance of being relieved, so he was compelled to surrender. The fall of Lathom House was regarded as an event of the first importance by the victors, and an order was issued by the House of Commons 'for the ministers about London to give public thanks to God, on the next Lord's Day for its surrender'. The seventh Earl of Derby subsequently fought with Charles II at Worcester when he was taken prisoner, and in due course was tried and beheaded. His widow, who features in Sir Walter Scott's *Peveril of the Peak*, survived until 1663, when she died at Knowsley.

2 Queen Henrietta Maria

England has not been lucky in her French queens, and Henrietta Maria was no exception. While Charles I lived no woman was apparently more devoted to her husband, for their early disagreements were merely those not unusual in a newly-married couple of different nationality, but she suffered from two very serious defects—she was extremely indiscreet and she was a very bad judge of character. Both of these characteristics were given full play when Charles had made his ill-advised attempt to arrest the Five Members.

The Queen had a close friend in the Countess of Carlisle, who, though Henrietta Maria was unaware of the fact, was the mistress of Pym, the most dangerous of the Parliamentary leaders. In fact, Lady Carlisle was an English version of the Duchesse de Chevreuse, and she breathed the very air of politics. When Charles had decided to go down to the House of Commons he had, somewhat inadvisedly, told his wife what he intended, but he had sworn her to secrecy, adding, 'If you find one hour elapse without hearing ill news of me, you will see me, when I return, the master of my kingdom.' The Queen, during that hour, had the greatest difficulty in controlling her impatience, although she was sitting with Lady Carlisle, who soon sensed that her mistress had something on her mind. As soon as the hour was up the Queen exclaimed in a tone of great excitement, 'Rejoice with me, for this hour the King is, as I have reason to hope, master of his realm, for Pym and his confederates are arrested before now'.

Unfortunately Lady Carlisle was possessed of considerable presence of mind, and while she went through the motions of registering delight at the news she took the first opportunity of leaving the room and sending a messenger down to the House of Commons to warn Pym to leave at once if the King had not already arrived; as it happened he had not, so that when he did arrive the birds had flown. Years later, when the Queen was dictating her reminiscences to that amiable old snob, Madame de Motteville, she admitted her part in what had taken place, but said of Charles's reaction, 'Never did he treat me for a moment with less kindness than before it happened though I had ruined him.'

Not long before the Civil War broke out the Queen went to the Continent to rally support for her husband, and during this period her mother, Marie de Medici, died. This caused her to write a letter to Charles in which she said, 'Forgive me for writing so badly, but I am distressed by the loss of the Queen my mother, who died a week ago, though I only had the news this morning. You must wear mourning, and all your suite, as well as the children.' The letter was typical of one who could only see a situation from a personal angle; for it never seems to have occurred to her that her husband had more serious matters on hand than formally grieving for the death of a mother-in-law whom he had never liked.

On the other hand the Queen was singularly successful in her efforts on behalf of Charles, and when she returned to England

early in 1643 she did so with a fleet of eleven vessels carrying
ammunition and other warlike supplies. They were convoyed by
the Dutch, who proved able to cope with the attentions of the
Parliamentary men-of-war but not with the weather, for the
crossing was one of the worst: it was then that Henrietta Maria
made her famous remark that queens of England were never
drowned. Whether this observation reassured the members of her
suite we have no means of knowing, but it is on record that during
the voyage they lost all reticence and insisted on confessing their
sins, in and out of season, at the tops of their voices, to the priests
who could hardly hear them above the thunder of the waves and
the crash of falling masts.

In due course the royal party arrived at Bridlington where the
Queen was soon surrounded by enthusiastic Royalists, among
whom was the Marquess of Montrose. He put a proposition to her
which, if it had been adopted, might have changed the whole
course of the war. He pointed out that things were going badly
for the King in Scotland, and he warned her that the Parliamentarians were already in negotiation with the Scots: if these two
parties came together the royal cause was lost. At the same time
the situation was not yet completely hopeless. If he, Montrose,
could be entrusted with the money and munitions which the
Queen had brought from the Continent he would rouse Scotland
for the King, and keep those who were his enemies there so
occupied at home that they would be unable to come to the assistance of the Parliamentarians south of the border.

Montrose, like Rupert, saw the war through the eyes of a
soldier—Henrietta Maria through those of a romantic woman. She
saw herself bringing aid to the King which would make him
emerge victorious, and, grateful for her help, he would in future
rely upon her advice to an even greater extent than in the past.
Of the dictates of sound strategy she knew nothing and cared less.
There was also a clash of personalities between her and Montrose.
She liked courtiers who flattered her facile optimism, while he
appeared brusque, and in actual fact he had little time for the sort
of quibbling in which she seemed to wish to indulge. Above all
it must never be forgotten that the Queen was the worst possible
judge of character, so she not only turned Montrose down, but
wrote him a letter from York which was equally tactless and
discourteous:

Cousin

I have received your letter, from which I understand that
you consider that things in Scotland are in a very bad state
as regards the King's interests, and that is due to my neglect
of certain proposals which were submitted to me on my
arrival here. As to that, I have obeyed the King's orders, but
I am still of the opinion that if the loyal supporters of the
King would only agree together and not waste time, all the
trouble which could be expected in that country would be
avoided. When the arms, which are coming from Denmark,
and expected daily, arrive you shall have all that you require,
and all the assistance in my power, for I still have great
confidence in you and in the generosity of your nature.

This confidence, I assure you, is in no way diminished,
though, like you, I have been greatly distressed by the
rumours that you had allied yourself with certain persons,
rumours well calculated to arouse apprehension in my breast.
But my confidence in you and the esteem in which I hold
you are not founded on such unstable grounds as casual
rumours, nor capable of being destroyed by something which,
if it happened as it has been reported, could only have
resulted from your zeal in the King's cause. Be assured that I
shall never fail in what I have promised you, and that I am
and shall remain

Your very good friend
Henriette Marie R.

What Montrose thought of this letter, with its obviously forced
cordiality and veiled hints of collusion with the Covenanters of
which he had been so wrongly accused, can only be imagined, but
it must have been extremely exasperating to a man who knew,
as he did, that if Scotland were to be gained for the King it must
be gained at once before the alliance between the Parliamentarians
and the Covenanters became an accomplished fact. Yet the
Queen's letter, for all its promises of help, told him that she
totally misunderstood the situation, and would obviously mis-
represent it to her husband when she reached Oxford. It was,
indeed, a gloomy thought.

Now that the Queen was about to march south to join her
husband it is not without interest to see what her relations with

Charles were at this particular time: of his devotion to her there
can be no doubt, but her attitude towards him is not so easy to
discover. Just before she left the Hague for England she had
written to him:

> Adieu, my dear heart; I expect either my life or death by the
> first tidings I shall receive from you, for if it happen that I
> could not come to you, it would be my death, since I can live
> no longer without seeing you. Believe this, for it is very true.

Nothing could be more typical of the devoted wife than this,
but it is difficult to reconcile with what we find her writing from
Bridlington on 3 April 1643:

> Hull is ours, and all Yorkshire, which is a thing to consider
> of: and for my particular if you make a peace, and disband
> your army before there is an end of this perpetual Parlia-
> ment, I am absolutely resolved to go to France, not being
> willing to fall again into the hands of these people, being
> well assured that if the power remains with them, it will not
> be well for me in England. Remember what I have written
> you in three precedent letters, and be more careful of me
> than you have been, or at least dissemble it. Adieu, the man
> hastens me, so that I can say no more.

This second letter betrays no sign of deep emotion.

From York the Queen marched south to Newark, and from there
she went by Ashby-de-la-Zouche, Crosshall, Waltham, and King's
Norton, with quite a considerable force:

> I carry with me 3,000 foot, 30 companies of horse and
> dragoons, 6 pieces of cannon, and two mortars, Henry
> Jermyn commands the forces which go with me as colonel
> of my guard, Sir Alexander Lesley the foot under him,
> Gerard the horse, and Robin Legge the artillery, and her
> she-majesty, generalissima over all, and extremely diligent
> am I, with 150 waggons of baggage to govern, in case of
> battle.

From Oxford the King was following her progress with the

closest interest and was taking every precaution for her safety, for there was always the possibility that Essex might try to arrest her progress:

Charles R.

Trusty and well-beloved we greet you well: whereas we have given directions to our dear nephew, Prince Rupert, to repair with a part of our forces, for the more secure conveying of our dearest Consort the Queen, in her passage to us, Our will and command is, that you and all officers under you, obey our said nephew as Commander-in-Chief, for which this shall be your orders.

Given at our Court at Oxford the 7th. July, 1643. To our trusty and well beloved Henry Jermyn, Esqr, Colonel of the Guards of our dearest Consort the Queen.

The relations between the Queen and Henry Jermyn became extremely close in later years, and some writers, notably Horace Walpole, have gone so far as to assert that they were lovers even before Henrietta Maria left England. However this may be, Jermyn certainly had an attraction for women. He sat in the House of Commons successively for Liverpool, Corfe Castle, and Bury St Edmunds, but he cut no great figure there: it was otherwise where the opposite sex were concerned, and for the seduction of a maid of honour he was for a time banished from Court, though it was not long before he wormed his way back as Master of the Horse. Had Charles known the manner of man Jermyn was, he would never have appointed him to the colonelcy of his wife's Guards.

Rupert was kept closely informed of the Queen's movements:

May it please your Highness

I am commanded by his Majesty to signify to your Highness that her Majesty will be this night at King's Norton in Worcestershire, and that (upon my Lord Capell's desire) his Majesty hath given my Lord Capell leave to return from there with all his forces (Colonel Sondis his regiments of horse and foot and my Lord Mountnorris horse excepted, which are to continue to attend her Majesty) into Shropshire and Cheshire for the safety of those parts, in case that her Majesty and your Highness do likewise and not otherwise.

Just now a messenger is come out of the West saying that Sir William Waller[4] hath fallen upon the Prince's rear, but hath lost a considerable number of horse and foot in the attempt, and my Lord Crauford was sent for with whose help it was expected that a period might be put to that business.

I remain
                    Your highness's most humble servant
                              Falkland

10 July
To complete the business of the
    West my Lord Wilmot with his
    Brigade marches immediately.

At Stratford-on-Avon the Queen met Rupert, and was also entertained for the night by Shakespeare's now widowed daughter, Susanna. From there she moved on to the valley of Keynton, near the foot of Edgehill, where Charles was waiting for her, and together they passed on to Oxford.

There she remained until the spring of the following year, and there is little to record of her activities, though it was during this period that her youngest child, Henrietta, later to be Duchess of Orleans, was conceived. When she arrived the military situation seemed promising enough, for the royal forces had been successful at Chalgrove Field, Atherton Moor, and Lansdown and Roundaway Down; Newcastle was in control of most of Yorkshire; and Rupert had taken Bristol: everything seemed to justify the Queen in her optimistic talk of a march on London and an early end to the war. The horizon, however, was soon to be clouded over, and as the months passed by the threat from the north became very serious. In August Montrose came to Oxford. Since he had spoken with the Queen at York he had exerted all his influence to keep Scotland neutral, and he now tried once more to warn the King of the danger that threatened him, but once more, and thanks largely to the influence of Henrietta Maria, no attention was paid to what he said.

    [4] b. 1597, d. 1668. Parliamentary general.

Yet while Montrose was vainly urging belated action, the General Assembly of the Church of Scotland was drawing up the Solemn League and Covenant by which members of the Reformed Religion would ally themselves with their co-religionists in the southern Kingdom: this was coupled with another document which arranged for the invasion of England by a force of 18,000 infantry, 2,000 cavalry, and 1,000 dragoons, supported by artillery, in consideration of a subsidy of £30,000 a month, instalments covering the first three months to be paid before the contingent moved. In pursuance of these arrangements a Scottish army entered England in January 1644; and it was not long before it became evident that the tide of war had changed, and that Oxford was no safe refuge for the Queen: so, on 3 April the King escorted his wife to Abingdon where they parted, never to meet again.

Years later, Henrietta Maria wrote to Charles II bitterly regretting the step she had taken:

> I have been the artificier of my misfortunes, for I ought never to have left the King my lord and husband, and your most loving father, since if I could not have prevented an end so disproportionate to the worth of such a king, at least I should have had the consolation of accompanying him to prison and the horrors of death . . . But you know, my dear son, what resistance I made to leave him, and that in my last adieus, embracing his royal knees, and supplicating your father and my lord not to permit this cruel separation, he raised me to his bosom and said: Madam, extreme remedies are requisite for extreme evils, and of two evils we must choose the least; where you to remain with me, which would be my greatest consolation, who would liberate me from the hands and snares of these ungrateful wretches, and who can procure me aid better than you? For mercy's sake, distress me no more by replying'. And I found myself ten leagues distant from him before I became conscious that I had left him.

When the Queen left Oxford she was in none too good a state of health. She was having a difficult pregnancy, and in addition she was suffering from a sort of rheumatic fever which some historians have attributed to her over-enthusiastic campaigning of the previous year: an old enemy in the shape of insomnia had also reappeared. She hoped that the waters at Bath might effect a cure, and from there she is found writing to the King:

> Fred Cornwallis will have told you all our voyage, as far as Axbury, and the state of my health since my coming hither; I find myself so ill, as well in the ill rest that I have, as in the increase of my rhume. I hope that this day's rest will do me good; I go to-morrow to Bristol, to send you back the carts; many of them are already returned. . . . Farewell, my dear heart, I cannot write more than that I am absolutely yours.

From Bath the Queen went to Exeter, where she hoped to be confined in peace and quiet, but her health continued to deteriorate, and she wrote to Sir Theodore Mayerne, an old man but one of the leading physicians of the day, who was living in London, beseeching him to come and look after her:

> Monsieur de Mayerne
>   My indisposition does not permit me to write much to beg you to come, if your health permit; but my disease will invite you more strongly, I hope, than many lines would do. Therefore I will only say this, having always in my recollection the care you have taken of me in my necessities, which makes me believe you will come if you can, and that l am, and ever shall be,
>   Your very good mistress and friend
>   Henriette Marie R.

Charles reinforced his wife's appeal with a single line:

> Mayerne
>   *Pour l'amour de moy allez trouver ma Femme.*
>   C.R.

This was at the beginning of May, and by the end of the month Mayerne was in Exeter, for the Parliament had provided him with the necessary permits to pass through territory by now largely under its control. He did not much approve of the Queen, and he regarded her as rather a silly woman, but she was his patient, and that was his first consideration. He found her in a very nervous state, but he was an outspoken man for a royal doctor, and he was far from believing that the best treatment was to humour her.

'Mayerne', she said, 'there are times when I think that I shall become distraught.'

'No reason to be afraid of that Madam', was the reply, 'You are distraught already.'

The baby arrived on 16 June, and was duly christened Henriette Anne after her mother and the Queen Regent of France: in spite of all the distractions which had preceded her birth she was to prove one of the most attractive of the Stuarts and, as 'Minette', to be the dearly-loved sister of Charles II. The worst of the Queen's troubles, however, was yet to come, for she was suffering from a classic case of puerperal sepsis. Her low state of health is very well shown in a letter she wrote to the King at this time:

My dear Heart
    Up to this time I was unwilling to trouble you with my complaints, having always hoped that time would remove my reasons for so doing, and because that would only grieve you: but when there is a probability of an increase of misery, it is well to prepare those whom we love to bear it. This then is what induces me to write you this letter, about my condition, which compels me to it by the violence of more ailments all at once, that either the state of my body, or that of my mind, depressed by the body, can support.
    Since I left you at Oxford, that disease which I began to feel there has constantly increased, but with attacks so violent as no one ever felt before. . . . And to render my condition complete, Essex has been threatening us with a siege, to which I cannot make up my mind and would rather set out on the road towards Falmouth, to pass from thence into France, if I can do it, even at the hazard of my life, than

stay here. I shall show you by this last action, that nothing
is so much in my thoughts as what concerns your preservation, and that my own life is of very little consequence compared with that; for as your affairs stand, they would be in
danger if you came to help me, and I know that your
affection would make you wish everything for that. This
makes me hazard my miserable life, a thing which in itself
is of very little consequence, excepting in so far as you value
it.

You will perhaps wish to know the particulars of my
disease; it is always a seizure of paralysis in the legs and all
over the body, but it seems to me as though my bowels and
stomach weigh more than a hundred pounds, and as though
I were so tightly squeezed in the region of the heart, that I
was suffocating; and at times I am like a person poisoned. I
can scarcely stir, and am doubled up. The same weight is
also upon my back; one of my arms has no feeling, and my
legs and knees are colder than ice. This disease has risen to
my head, I cannot see with one eye. It has pleased God
to prove me, both in body and mind. I trust in His goodness
that he will not abandon me, and He will give me
patience.

Adieu, my dear heart. . . .

The most miserable creature in the world, who can write
no more.

From my bed, this 28th. June. Exeter.

Whether this was a considerate letter to write to one who had
so many cares as Charles must be a matter of opinion, and it
certainly strengthens the views of those of her critics who contend
that she always thought of herself first.

That she was ill admits of no doubt, and Mayerne advised her
to return to Bath, where not only the waters but the general
peace and quiet would be calculated to have a soothing effect upon
her nervous system. It would, however, mean crossing the Roundhead lines, but no great difficulty was anticipated on that score,
for even the Westminster Parliament had put no obstacle in the
way of Mayerne going to her from London. So she applied for a
safe conduct to Essex, whom she had known since she first came
to England at the time of her marriage: he had filled various

offices at court, including that of Lord Chamberlain, and although he had taken the side of the Parliament in the Civil War she credited him with being enough of a gentleman not to refuse her request.

Bad judge of character as always, she had mistaken her man. The ex-husband of Frances Howard and Elizabeth Paulet was not going to neglect this opportunity of revenging himself on James I in the person of his daughter-in-law, so in reply to the Queen's appeal he wrote a letter loyally signifying his willingness to escort her to London, where she would have the best medical attention, and where her presence was anyhow required to answer to Parliament for having levied war on England. Essex knew, and so did Henrietta Maria, that this was an invitation to be murdered, though doubtless under the form of law, but, so far as he cared, she might stop at Exeter and be killed by one of his cannon balls. What the Countess of Derby had said about the tender mercies of the wicked was also proving true in the case of the Earl of Essex.

This ungracious epistle seems to have roused the Queen to action, for she contrived to get out of Exeter and went to Pendennis Castle, from where she wrote to her husband:

My dear Heart
   This letter is to bid you adieu. If the wind is favourable, I shall set off to-morrow. Henry Seymour will tell you many things from me, which the miserable condition in which I am does not permit me to write. I beg you to send him to me again to France, where, if God grant me grace to recover my health, I hope yet to serve you . . . Adieu, my dear heart. If I die, believe that you will lose a person who has never been other than entirely yours.

Soon after writing this letter the Queen succeeded in making her escape to France, disguised as a country woman, leaving her baby in the care of Lady Dalkeith: she landed on the coast of Brittany not far from Brest, and went on to Bourbon where she took the waters instead of at Bath.

Her letters to Charles soon produced an effect for, believing her to be in danger at Exeter, he stormed down to the south-west, raised the siege of the Devonshire town, and compelled the

surrender of Essex's army at Lostwithiel, though the Earl himself
managed to escape. For the King, however, the victory was a
Pyrrhic one, for he missed the Queen by ten days, but in the eyes
of the world the discmofiture of Essex went a long way to reverse
the verdict of Marston Moor fought on 2 July.

While the King and Queen were together at Oxford naturally
no letter passed between them, so the counsels which Henrietta
Maria pressed on her husband can only be surmised, but once she
had left the country it becames possible to trace the direction in
which her influence was exercised. For example on 17 January
1645, we find her writing from Paris:

My dear Heart

Tom Elliott, two days since, hath brought me much joy
and sorrow; the first, to know the good estate you are in; the
other, the fear I have that you go to London. I cannot conceive where the wit was of those that gave you this counsel,
unless it be to hazard your person to save theirs. But, thanks
be to God, to-day I received one of yours by the ambassador
of Portugal, dated in January, which comforted me much to
see that the treaty shall be at Uxbridge. For the honour of
God, trust not yourself in the hands of those people. If ever
you go to London before the Parliament be ended, or without a good army, you are lost. I understand that the propo-
sitions for peace must begin by disbanding your army. If
you consent to this you are lost; they having the whole power
of the militia, they have and will do whatsoever they will.

I received yesterday letters from the Duke of Lorraine
who sends me word, that if his services be agreeable, he will
bring you 10,000 men. Dr. Goffe, whom I have sent into
Holland, shall treat with him in his passage upon this
business, and I hope very speedily to send you good news of
this, as also of the money. Assure yourself I shall be wanting
nothing you can desire, and that I will hazard my life—that
is, I will die with famine rather than not send it to you.
Send me word, always, by whom you receive my letters, for
I write both by the ambassador of Portugal and the resident
of France. Above all, have a care not to abandon those who
have served you, as well the bishops as the poor Catholics.
Adieu.

The end of the year saw Charles in negotiation with the Scots to whom, contrary to the advice of Rupert, he was soon to entrust himself. However, he was still at Oxford, and from there he wrote to the Queen on 4 January 1646:

Dear Heart

I desired thee to take notice that with the year I begin to new number my letters, hoping to begin a year's course of good luck. I have heard of but seen no letters from thee since Christmas Day; the reason is evident, for an intelligence with the Portugal's agent is obstructed, so that I am not so confident as I was that any of my letters will come safe to thee. But methinks, if Cardinal Mazarin were by half so kind to us as he professes to be, it would be no great difficulty for him to secure our weekly intelligence. And in earnest I desire thee to put him to it, for besides that, if the efforts of it succeed, it will be of great consequence to me, I shall very much judge of the reality of his intentions according to his answer in this.

If Ashburnham complain to thee of my wilfulness, I am sure it is that way which at least thou wilt excuse, if not justify in me; but, if thou hadst seen a former paper (to which being but an accessory I must not blame his judgement), thou woud'st have commended my choleric rejection of it, the aversion to which it is possible (though I will not confess it until thou sayest so) might have made me too nice in this, of which I will say no more; but consider well that which I sent in the place of it, and then judge.

My great officers are so much in expectation that for the present I can give thee but little account of them, albeit yet in conjecture (as I believe) that the rebels will not admit of my personal treaty at London, and I hope well of having 2,000 foot and horse, out of my smaller garrisons. As for the Scots, we yet have no news of them, neither concerning this treaty, nor of that which I have begun with David Lesley. And, lastly, that the Duke of York's journey is absolutely broken both in respect of the loss of Hereford, as that of the relief of Chester is yet but very doubtful. But upon this design, having commanded Sir George Radcliffe[5] to wait

[5] b. 1593, d. 1657.

upon him, I desire thy approbation that he may be sworn
gentleman of his bedchamber, for which, though he be very
fit, and I assure thee that he is far from being a Puritan, and
that it will be much for my son's good to have him settled
about him, yet I would not have him sworn without thy
consent.

So God bless thee, sweetheart

Charles R.

Even now Montreuil is come hither concerning this treaty.
The Queen cannot have a particular account of it till my
next.

Jean de Montreuil was an agent of the French government who
was endeavouring to bring about an arrangement between Charles
and the Scots, which the Queen very much favoured. The stum-
bling-block was religion, for the Scots wished the King to assent
to the establishment of Presbyterianism in England, which he
refused to do, much to Henrietta Maria's annoyance: indeed, there
was a definite rift at this time between husband and wife on the
point, as the following letter clearly proves:

Oxford, January 14, 1646.

Dear Heart

I had no time before Friday last to decipher thine of the
25th. of November, which I must answer how late soever,
(for kindness is never out of date), every line in it being a
several way of expressing thy love to me, even there where
we differ in judgement, which I know we should not do if
thou wert not mistaken in the state of the question; I
mean concerning Episcopacy, for I am of thy opinion to a
tittle in everything else.

For the difference between me and the rebels concerning
the Church is not bare matter of form or ceremony, which
are alterable according to occasion, but so real, that if I should
give way as is desired, here would be no Church, and by
human probability ever to be recovered; so that, besides the
obligation of mine oath, I know nothing to be on higher
point of conscience. This being granted, I am sure thy persua-
sions will be turned into praises of my constancy. And for

50

the truth of my affection, the doubt of which is the only argument against me, I can make it as clear to any not wilful person, as two and three makes five. But this I am sure of, which none can deny, that my yielding this is a sin of the highest nature, if I believe constant as I have said, which really I do.

And dear heart, thou canst not but be confident that there is no danger which I will not hazard, or pains that I will not undergo, to enjoy the happiness of thy company, there being nothing which really conduceth thereunto which I will not do, which may not make me less worthy of thee. And to this end I prosecute the Scotch treaty with all the industry and dexterity which God hath given me, not differing in opinion concerning it. My intended journey to London is likewise for this. Than which, believe me, no undertaking can be less hazardous (the greatest fear of my doing some *lache* action which thy love will hinder thee to apprehend and mine to give the occasion), nor of so great probability of good success. One of my securities I forgot in my last to mention to thee, which is, that this Parliament without doubt determines with my life, if I give it not some new additional strength, which I protest never to do, but for the contrary, to follow precisely thy advice therein.

> So God bless thee, sweetheart
> Charles R.

Her husband's arguments had no effect upon the Queen who was still urging him to save himself by the sacrifice of the Church. As in the case of Rupert, the King looked upon the struggle in a totally different light, and to the Queen, who as a Catholic saw no profound difference between one form of heresy and another, his attitude was quite incomprehensible considering the secular issues at stake: it was in these circumstances that Charles returned to the charge.

> Oxford, February 19, 1646

Dear Heart

Albeit that my personal danger must of necessity precede thine, yet thy safety seems to be hazarded by my resolution concerning Church government. I am doubly grieved to

51

differ with thee in opinion, though I am confident that my judgement, not love is censured by thee for it. But I hope, whatsoever thou mayst wish, thou wilt not blame me at all, if thou rightly understand the state of the question. For I assure thee, I put little or no difference between setting up the Presbyterian government, or submitting to the Church of Rome. Therefore make the case thine own. With what patience wouldst thou give ear to him who should persuade thee, for worldy respects, to leave the communion of the Roman Church for any other? Indeed, sweetheart, this is my case, for suppose my concession in this should prove but temporary, it may palliate though not excuse my sin.

But it is strange to me how that can be imagined, not remembering any example that concessions in this kind have been recalled, which in this case is more unlikely (if not impossible) than any other, because the means of recovering it is destroyed in the first minute of yielding, it being not only a condition for my assistance, but likewise all the eclesiastical power so put in their hands, who are irreconcilable enemies to that government which I contend for, as I shall never be able to master.

I must confess (to my shame and grief) that heretofore I have for public respects (yet I believe, if thy personal safety had not been at stake, I might have hazarded the rest) yielded unto those things which were no less against my conscience than this, for which I have been so deservedly punished, that a relapse now would be insufferable, and I am most confident that God hath so favoured my hearty (though weak) repentance, that He will be glorified, either by relieving me out of these distresses (which I may humbly hope for, though not presume upon), or in my gallant sufferings for so good a cause, which to eschew by any mean submission cannot but draw God's further justice upon me, both in this and the next world. But let not this sad discourse trouble thee (for, as thou art free from my faults, so doubtless God hath blessings in store for thee), it being only a necessary freedom to show thee, that no slight cause can make me deny to do what thou desirest, who am eternally thine,

Charles R.

For God's sake, as thou lovest me see what may be done
for the landing of the 5,000 men, at the place and by the
time as I wrote to thee the 1st. of February, and with them
as much money as possibly thou canst. I assure thee that
the welldoing of this is likely to save both my crown and
liberty.

The letters which the King and the Queen were exchanging at
this time are evidence both of the straits to which the Royalist
cause had been reduced, and of their own failure to realize their
real position. It was a fundamental error to suppose that foreign
governments would come to their assistance when there was
nothing to be gained in return, while the arrival of a horde of
ruffians from the battle-fields of the Thirty Years' War would
have neutralized, by the alienation of the British people, any
military assistance they might have brought: any help that the
Pope, to whom Charles also turned, might give would not have
been worth the discredit of asking him for it.

Only in the south-west did the King possess even the semblance
of an army. Goring had resigned his command there in the
previous November, and had retired to France: his second-in-
command was Sir Richard Grenville, 'in whom', it has been well
said, 'the demoniac strain that ran through all the Grenvilles was
tempered by no finer quality, and who, with his ferocious rapacity,
was a greater terror to the hitherto loyal countryside than he was
to the enemy', In January 1646 the Prince of Wales and his
councillors nominated Hopton as commander-in-chief, and it was
resolved to attempt the relief of Exeter which was again besieged,
but when Hopton with not more than 9,000 men reached Torrington he heard that Fairfax was approaching.

All the same he determined to make a fight for it, so he proceeded to throw up barricades at the entrance to the town, and
placed a party of dragoons a mile to the east; but the advancing
Roundheads soon drove in this outpost, whereupon the Cavaliers
withdrew into Torrington itself. Fairfax then sent Oliver Cromwell, who was serving under his orders, to reconnoitre the position, and from the noise coming from the town the latter deduced
that Hopton was on the point of retiring. To test this assumption
Cromwell sent forward a patrol of dragoons, and an affair of out-
posts developed into a general action. 'The dispute continued

long at push of pike and with butt-ends of muskets', wrote Fairfax, but in the end the Royalists broke: the Cavalier horse then counter-attacked in an effort to restore the situation, and in the confusion the Royalist magazine, which was situated in the church, blew up, when Fairfax himself narrowly escaped with his life. All the same, in the end the Royalists were driven out of the town.

As a result of the loss of Torrington the shadow of defeat now fell over the remaining Royalist forces in the south-west. Hopton retreated through Cornwall, but his army was steadily dwindling owing to desertion, so that on 14 March he felt compelled to surrender to Fairfax at Tressilian bridge near Truro, by which time the Prince of Wales had already left the mainland for the Scilly Isles. The last Royalist force in the west having been eliminated in this way, Fairfax turned back upon Exeter, where the governor, by this time hopeless of relief by sea or land, surrendered the city on 9 April. This was followed by the surrender of all the fortresses in the west that still held out for Charles, with the exception of Pendennis Castle.

One person still refused to give way to despair, and that was the King himself. He still believed that Ireland would supply him with some 10,000 men, and he ignored the fact that by now every port in England and Wales was in the possession of the Parliament, so there was nowhere they could land if they did come—a fact of which the Irish themselves were only too well aware and which made them extremely reluctant to run upon what was clearly certain destruction. Charles for a brief space placed hopes in the efforts of the Queen to secure the landing of the 5,000 men mentioned in his letter, and he resolved to muster every available man, break out from Oxford, and join these auxiliaries. In obedience to orders to this effect, Astley[6] drew 3,000 men from the remaining garrisons in the region of the Severn, and marched in the direction of Oxford; but near Stow-on-the-Wold he was defeated by a Parliamentary force, and a week later, on the news of Hopton's surrender, Astleys' men followed his example. Their commander sat himself on a drum in the midst of his captors to whom he said, somewhat prophetically, 'You have done your work, and may go play, unless you will fall out amongst yourselves.' It was the end.

[6] b. 1579, d. 1652.

The King now had three alternatives open to him if he wished to avoid the ignominy of being captured in Oxford, towards which Fairfax was now approaching—he could surrender to the Scots, entrust himself to the Parliament, or take refuge abroad. Strangely enough it was to the last of these options, which in retrospect would appear to have been the most attractive, that he gave the least consideration. The differences between the various sections of his conquerors had already progressed so far as to foreshadow their disruption, which would have been accelerated by the disappearance of the King, and the schisms which developed after his execution would have taken place after his flight. Had he adopted this course he could hardly have failed to be restored after a few years. Admittedly he could not have foreseen with any accuracy the course which events were likely to take, but to hand himself over to the Scots or the Parliament was indeed a counsel of despair.

To the very last he seems to have been undecided which line he should take, as the following letter to the Prince of Wales abundantly proves:

Oxford, March 22, 1646

Charles

Hoping that this will find you safe with your mother, I think fit to write this short but necessary letter to you. Then know, that your being where you are, safe from the power of the rebels, is, under God, either my greatest security, or my certain ruin. For, your constancy to religion, obedience to me, and to the rules of honour, will make these insolent men begin to hearken to reason, when they shall see their injustice not like to be crowned with quiet. But, if you depart from these grounds, for which I have all this time fought, then your leaving the kingdom will be (with too much probability) called sufficient proofs for many of the slanders heretofore laid upon me.

Wherefore, once again I command you, upon my blessing, to be constant to your religion, without hearkening to Roman superstitions nor the seditious and schismatical doctrines of the Presbyterians and Independents. For I know that a persecuted Church is not thereby less pure, though less fortunate. For all other things, I command you to be totally directed by your mother; and, as subordinate to her, by the remainder of that council which I put to you at your parting from thence.

> And so, God bless you.
> Charles R.

Four days later he seems to have made up his mind to entrust his fortunes to the Parliament, for he wrote to Lord Digby:

> Oxford, March 26, 1646.
> I am endeavouring to get to London so that the conditions may be such as a gentleman may own, and that the rebels may acknowledge me as King, being not without hope that I shall be able to draw either the Presbyterians or Independents to side with me, for extirpating the one or the other, that I shall be really King again.
>
> Howsoever, I desire you to assure all my friends that, if I cannot live as a King, I shall die like a gentleman, without doing that which make honest men blush for me.

On the evening of 26 April he told his council definitely that he was going to London, and authorized them to surrender Oxford if they did not hear of him in three weeks. Next morning he rode out of Oxford disguised as a servant in attendance on Ashburnham and Dr Hudson, one of his chaplains. They took the London road, but when they reached Hillingdon in Middlesex the King seems to have changed his mind: after some hesitation he turned northwards, and sent Hudson to Montreuil who was staying at Southwell, with the request that he would obtain satisfactory written assurances from the Scots. Early on 5 May Charles himself reached Southwell, and from then he was never a free man again.

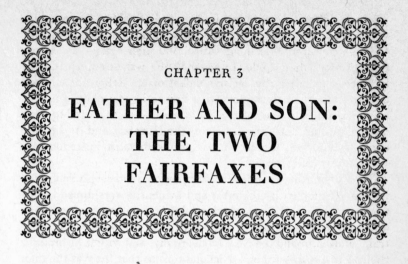

CHAPTER 3

FATHER AND SON: THE TWO FAIRFAXES

On the Parliamentary side the outstanding figures in the period covered by the papers in the possession of Colonel Alan Dower were the Lords Fairfax, father and son: this is not to say that Oliver Cromwell was not working his way up all the time, but he did not reach pre-eminence, or anything approaching it, until later in the war: during these earlier years he was, at least nominally, under the command of Sir Thomas Fairfax—the limelight came later.

The Fairfaxes were a Yorkshire family, and Ferdinando, the second Lord, was born in 1584. He espoused the Parliamentary side when the Civil War broke out and, with the cloth towns of the West Riding to back him, he was able to prevent the Royalist armies in the north of England under the Earl of Newcastle from marching south to join the King for the advance on London. All the same he seems to have been a somewhat colourless, and certainly not an inspiring, individual, for although he did none too badly at Hull he abandoned his own son at Adwalton Moor and at Marston Moor he abandoned his army.

His son, Sir Thomas Fairfax, was a very different character. He had been born in 1611, and had served in the Low Countries in his earlier years. As a soldier he believed in taking the offensive whenever possible, as he showed early in the war, when in May 1643 he captured Wakefield with 1,500 men against an enemy force of more than 2,000. In adversity he was as enterprising as in success, for after the decisive defeat of his father and himself at Adwalton Moor in the following month he was obliged to seek refuge behind the walls of Hull: all the same he managed to ferry a large number of his cavalry across the Humber, and in this way enabled Cromwell to check a dangerous Royalist incursion into Lincolnshire at Winceby.

Thomas Fairfax was quiet, modest, serious, and deeply religious; he was popular with all ranks; and evidently worshipped by his troops. In effect, he possessed an impressive stock of military qualities, so it is hardly surprising that he was selected to form, train, and command the New Model Army, and with it he brought the war to a successful end. Nicholas tells us that 'he was the man most beloved and trusted by the rebels', while Whitelocke[1] testifies that, though modest and diffident in council, yet in action 'he was so highly transported that scarce any man dare speak to him'. The almost feminine cast of features in his earlier portraits gives no indication of such a temperament, though the later ones show a more martial and virile personality. His strength or weakness of character will be discussed on a later page.
He early showed the offensive spirit:

May it please your Lordship
These parts grows very impatient of our delay in beating them out at Leeds and Wakefield, for by them all trade and provisions are stopt so that the people in these clothering towns are not able to subsist, and indeed so pressing is their wants as some hath told me if I would not stir with them they must rise of necessity themselves: in a thing of so great importance I thought it fit to acquaint you with it, to desire your Lordship's advice before I would undertake it, therefore humbly desire your Lordship not to defer this business, but if no aid can come to us, then to give us advice and order what to do; for long this country can not subsist and to raise the country to assault the enemy—I would not do it without your Lordship's consent being only commanded to defend

[1] b. 1605, d. 1675. Keeper of the Great Seal

the ports from them. I desire with all speed this bearer may bring us your Lordship's resolution.

I am sure I shall have above six hundred muskets if I summons the country to come in beside the thousand or more with other weapons that would rise with us if your Lordship please to give me power to join with the readiness of the people I doubt not but by God's assistance to give your Lordship a good account of what we do. So humbly desiring your blessing, I will ever be

Your Lordship's most
obedient son
Tmo. Fairfax

Bradford, Jan. 9. 1642.
    For the right Honble.
        my honored father
        the Lord Fairfax.

In the following year a letter from Sir John Hotham is further proof that father and son were already the driving force behind the Parliamentary cause in the north of England:

May it please your Lordship

I received your letter, and do intend to fulfil your commands with all expedition. I am now marched up to Nottingham and Colonel Cromwell's forces with me; here is Lord Grey come too, and this day we expect Sir John Gill; Sir William Brereton[2] hath order to draw down to us, then we shall be strong. The Manchester forces have orders to draw down to you, and furnish you with what you want. I shall endeavour all I can to join with you, or otherwise to distress the enemy. Our misery is, we know not where his force lies, nor in what condition he is. I shall desire to have some information from you on that point, and I shall not fail to endeavour that which may be best for the public service, and will ever remain

Your lordship's humble servant
John Hotham

Nottingham, May 24th., 1643
For the Right Hon. Ferdinando Lord Fairfax
    General of the Northern Forces, these present.

[2] b. 1604, d. 1661. Parliamentary commander.

Hotham was the man who had closed the gates of Hull in the King's face at the beginning of the war. He was MP for Beverley, and an old campaigner of the Thirty Years' War. We are told that he was a person of unpleasing manners and ungovernable temper, while he seems to have had no very decided allegiance except to the main chance: this was in the end to cause him to try to double-cross his Parliamentary associates, for which they duly put him to death.

The entry of the Scottish army into England in January 1644 gave the Fairfaxes, father and son, their chance, for it compelled the Royalist commander, Newcastle, to divide his forces, and so enabled Thomas Fairfax to defeat Bellasys[3] at Selby. On 2 July of that same year came the decisive victory of Marston Moor which ruined the King's cause north of the Humber, and as a result Fairfax gained such a reputation by his gallant conduct and prudent tactics that on 21 January 1645, by a vote of the House of Commons, he was appointed Commander-in-Chief of the New Model Army. This had to no small extent been due to a clash in the previous December between the two Houses at Westminster, which resulted in the so-called Self-Denying Ordinance:

My Lord

During my being within doors, I forbore your Lordship's trouble. In this kind be pleased now to pardon me in the receiving of my acknowledgements of all respect and service. Your lordship will, from many hands, have heard of a vote passed your House, that no member of either should have any office, civil or martial, during these civil wars; and for the trial, that will not be partial, it was this day carried, that my Lord of Essex should not be excepted out of that Ordinance.

Two things upon this occasion I may safely say, that I would to God we had such a successor in all other places as your lordship will have, and that further than your lordship is generally involved in the Vote, you are not otherwise concerned or intended in it that I ever heard of. This being so, if this Ordinance pass the Houses, your case will be with honour and comfort, for a general good, to resign your command over unto him who is properly to inherit and will

3 b. 1614, d. 1689.

60

constantly make good all the honour you can leave him. By the letter inclosed you will see what is the King's answer, and what upon the delivery of it was said by my Lord Duke of Richmond.

I am your lordship's most humble servant
P. Wharton[4]

December 17th., 1644
For my Lord Fairfax at York.

By the end of April the Committee of Both Kingdoms, which controlled the movements of the Parliamentary forces, decided that the New Model was ready to take the field, and Fairfax was ordered to relieve Taunton, a task which he duly accomplished on 11 May. His next assignment was to besiege Oxford itself, but this he felt to be unsound strategy:

May it please your Lordship

I am very sorry we should spend our time unprofitably before a town, whilst the King hath time to strengthen himself, and by terror to force obedience of all places where he comes; the Parliament is sensible of this now, therefore hath sent me directions to raise the siege and march to Buckingham, where, I believe, I shall have orders to advance northwards, in such a course as all our divided parties may join.

It is the earnest desire of the army to follow the King, but the endeavours of others to prevent it hath so much prevailed; but I trust God will preserve it to do the public service: to-morrow I begin my march (God willing). If your Lordship strengthen York and Hull, I trust they shall not have time to besiege any places; so beseeching God to keep your Lordship in health, and those parts in safety, desiring your blessing, I rest,

Your Lordship's most obedient son
Thomas Fairfax

Marston, 4th. June, 1645.
For the Right Honble. the Lord Fairfax
    Lord General of the North

[4] b. 1613, d. 1696.

On the day after he had written this letter, Fairfax broke camp
from before Oxford, and marched north-east to Newport Pagnell.
On 8 June his Council of War decided to make the royal army its
main objective rather than waste its energies on outlying garrisons,
and it gave Fairfax a completely free hand in the conduct of his
operations, while Cromwell was appointed as his second-in-
command. On the 14th he won the decisive battle of Naseby,
when, like Wellington at Waterloo, he seems to have been every-
where he was wanted.

Few battles in the Civil War have been subject to so much
misrepresentation. In actual fact, apart from the generalship of
Fairfax, the Roundhead victory was largely due to the disastrous
decision of the King to allow Goring with three thousand cavalry
to move off to the west, in consequence of which there was a
greater disparity in numbers than at any other major battle of the
war—it was a blunder comparable with that of Napoleon in
detaching Grouchy on the eve of Waterloo. Thus the popular
belief that the Roundhead victory was primarily due to the
creation of the New Model is as ill-founded as the equally popular
belief that Cromwell was its creator: the majority of the Parliamentary foot at Naseby were conscripts.

Fairfax made no attempt to follow up his victory, but besieged
Leicester, which fell to him on 18 June. Many historians have
taken the line that he was a better tactician than strategist, but
those who have expressed this view have been inclined to forget
that his tactics were his own, while his strategy was as often as
not dictated to him by the Committee of Both Kingdoms. So with
Leicester in his pocket he set off to raise the siege of Taunton,
which was sustaining a heroic defence under Admiral Blake[5]
against Goring. Fairfax, like Rupert and Montrose, could move
with a speed remarkable in seventeenth-century warfare when
circumstances demanded, and so it proved on this occasion. On
Monday 30 June the forced march began from Marlborough:
twenty miles were covered the first day, and the Roundheads
billeted in Amesbury that night. Next day they moved on to
Stonehenge, and then south-west to Bower Chalk, seven miles
west of Salisbury: on Wednesday they reached Blandford, and by
Friday night they were at Beaminster, having come by way of
Dorchester. This represented a five days' march of seventeen

[5] b. 1599, d. 1657.

miles a day, and in hot weather, but at the end of it Fairfax was greeted with the unexpected news that Goring had suddenly abandoned the siege of Taunton and was on the way to Yeovil.

With Cromwell as his second-in-command Fairfax decided to follow him, and he was the better able to do so for, at this juncture, he was joined by another Roundhead army under Edward Massey, so on 10 July there took place at Langport one of the last battles of the Civil War, which resulted in a brilliant victory for Fairfax.

Admittedly this was one of the occasions when his strategy was not impressive while that of Goring was masterly, but tactically there can be nothing but admiration for Fairfax's handling of the battle. This is not the place for a detailed account of the actual fighting, but though his action in launching a cavalry force four abreast through a defile commanded by the enemy's fire may appear almost foolhardy, it succeeded, and that is always the acid test. Once more Fairfax proved that he could guess correctly what was 'on the other side of the hill'. In effect, he calculated accurately the relative forces and values of the two sides, and his experience and judgment of war served him in good stead. At the same time, it must be admitted that his victory was in no small measure due to the King's inactivity, for Charles made no effort to take the pressure off Goring, but hung about Hereford and Raglan from 19 June to 15 July.

After this victory Fairfax set out methodically to subdue the west, and the capture of Bridgwater on 23 July gave him the line of the Parrett. He then struck at Bristol:

May it please Your Lordship

Upon serious debate on the consequence of affairs, we marched to Bristol with the army, else the good success God hath given us in Somersetshire might have been to little purpose; for Prince Rupert, with 3,000 horse and foot which he had, might have raised force in all the country behind us, which would have been more considerable than Goring's army is, which breaks daily with desertions, and so less dangerous.

We have shut Prince Rupert, with all his horse, up in Bristol: the plague is much there. I hope God will direct all things for the best, that we may give some good account of

that which is so much expected. So, desiring your blessing,
I remain,

Your Lordship's most obedient son

Thomas Fairfax

For the Right Honble. the Lord Fairfax.[6]

The circumstances attendant upon Rupert's surrender of Bristol
and their aftermath have been discussed on an earlier page, but
in view of the King's charges against his unfortunate nephew it
may be recalled here that the Parliamentary Colonel, Butler,
gave it as his opinion that Rupert could not have held the town
'unless it had been better manned'.

With Bristol in his hands Fairfax kept up the pressure on the
Royalists in the west. He met with particularly stout resistance at
Sherborne, Devizes, and Berkeley Castle, but he overcame it all
the same, and by the end of December he was at Crediton. In the
meantime he had detached Cromwell to mop up the King's
garrisons in Hampshire, a task which he accomplished most
efficiently, giving at Basing House a foretaste of that savagery
which he was later to display on a more extended scale during his
Irish campaign. Of course much of the Roundhead success was
due to the demoralization of their opponents, for even Hyde went
so far as to describe the once formidable Royalist cavalry as 'horse
whom only their friends feared and their enemies laughed at,
being only terrible in plunder and resolute in running away'. As
has already been shown, the end came at the beginning of April
the following year with the surrender of Exeter itself.

With the events of the rest of 1646 Fairfax had little to do, and
it is clear that he found public affairs more than a little perplexing:

May it please Your Lordship

I thought it fit to discharge this duty of writing to your
Lordship, though I have little from hence to advertise you
of. By this the convoy is at York. I sent with it three
regiments of horse, three regiments of foot, and five hundred
dragoons. This number, I hope, will prevent jealousies, and
yet be sufficient to secure their charge. Twelve thousand
pounds is sent down with these that they might discharge
their quarters.

[6] This letter is undated, but it was clearly written in August 1645.

I have not now much business here; yet I conceive it fit to be with the army till the Scots be marched out of the kingdom, or on their march.

I hear my wife intends to come to Northampton. I know not whether I should advise her to stay, or not; but if she come, her own trouble will be more than any inconvenience of the journey. Though now it hath pleased God, in some good measure, to settle the general affairs of the kingdom, I should be glad to settle mine own in some more certainty. but till I see how it may please God, further to dispose of me; but I must confess that neither myself nor any with me can advise me what is the best course to take in this thing, the public business being wholly taken up my thoughts, making me a stranger to my own business, and that, I most fear, to my nearest and dearest friends. I hope the Lord will direct me what to do, or willingly to obey whatsoever your Lordship shall advise or command me, who am

Your Lordship's most obedient son
T. Fairfax

Northampton, Dec. 30th. 1646

I humbly present my service to my Lady.

For the Right Hon. my honoured Father

The Lord Fairfax.

The convoy, to which Sir Thomas Fairfax alludes, was that carrying the money with which to discharge the outstanding debts of the Parliament to the Scots. On 30 January of the following year the first £100,000 was paid to the Scots, whereupon they surrendered Newcastle, and on 3 February a second like sum was paid, when they gave up whatever other fortresses they held, and re-crossed the border, at the same time delivering Charles to commissioners appointed by the English Parliament, who took him to Holmby House in Northamptonshire.

Fairfax was soon to know how it pleased God to dispose of him, and it was to play a part for which he was by no means well suited. Three days before the King reached Holmby, Fairfax came up from the south, met him at Nottingham and paid his homage, going on one knee, and kissing his hand: it was then that Charles made the remark that Fairfax was a man of honour. So he may have appeared to the King, who was not a good judge of character anyhow, but he was not a man of backbone, for although he was Cromwell's superior officer he was as wax in his hands, as events were soon to show.

By this time there had widened a considerable gulf between the Parliament and the army which was nominally its servant, but in reality its master, and it can hardly be denied that the soldiers had considerable grievances. Before the end of March 1647 their arrears of pay had become quite intolerable, for eighteen months' was due to the infantry, and to the cavalry and dragoons forty-three weeks'—the total amount being half as much again as had been paid to the Scots. There was no provision for pensions to the widows of those who had been killed, and there was none for keeping the soldiers in food and lodging, so there was continuous friction with the civilians on whom they were billeted. Such was the way in which the victorious army of the Parliament was treated when it had only recently seen the Scots bought off before its eyes. The Parliament was well aware of the situation, and was working towards the disbandment of the army as the ideal solution, while the military leaders were moving in the direction of a *coup d'état*. In these circumstances it was clear that the control of the person of the King would be a factor of considerable strength to the party which could secure it.

Hilaire Belloc has advanced the interesting theory that there was a strong additional force making for antagonism between Parliament and the army, and that was class feeling. 'The Parliamentarians', he says, 'were most of them gentlemen. The colonels of the army were some of them, by this time, men risen by talent or brutality from lower ranks of society, and the subaltern officers were often of such origin.'

However this may be, Fairfax and Cromwell decided that the time had come to act. The former at once disobeyed his orders, and concentrated the army at Newmarket instead of disbanding it, while Cromwell went even further and, unknown to Fairfax, called a meeting of a few carefully-chosen officers at his house in Drury Lane, where it was decided to send a Cornet Joyce to Holmby and remove Charles from the custody of the Parliament into that of the army: this decision having been taken, Cromwell rapidly removed himself from London, where the Parliament was in control, as he had no desire to meet the fate of Strafford. How completely these arrangements were made behind the back of

Fairfax is proved by the fact that Joyce was actually an officer in his bodyguard.

His headquarters were at Newmarket, and when he heard what had taken place he was horrified; while he had been forced into a situation over which he had no control, and which he had been desperately striving to avoid. As soon as the news reached him he sent a Colonel Whalley,[7] who was a cousin of Cromwell, with a body of horse to restore the King to the custody of the Parliamentary Commissioners, but Charles refused to do what he was asked, and Whalley probably knew enough of Cromwell's designs to realize that it would be inadvisable to press him. At this point Fairfax and Cromwell met the King at a house on the outskirts of Cambridge where he had been staying, and both men assured him that they were not responsible for Joyce's action, in saying which Fairfax was telling the truth and Cromwell was telling a lie. However, Charles refused to be returned to the Commissioners for reasons of his own which are none too easy to follow, but which suited Cromwell very well, so he was taken south still in the custody of the army.

My Lord

I must crave your pardon for my brevity. I hope Mr. Bowles will enlarge. Things are mighty uncertain, rather tending to a confusion than composing of differences. The General is commanded down to the army: one saying in the House he had time enough to go to Hyde Park, but not to attend his duty—speaking it with much scorn.

Truly, my Lord, it is resolved upon the question that nothing but exasperation and provocation shall be used to enforce the army to disorder. And then the Presbyterians say they are necessitated to join with the King; and in order to this design, the King hath sent up to the Parliament his answer to the proposition to settle Presbytery for three years, the militia for ten years, and such like. A committee is appointed to consider of the King's answer. It is well for Your Lordship to be absent; for it is in vain to be here. And were it not for the good of the kingdom, were I as the General, I would scorn to hold my command an hour longer;

---

[7] Subsequently a regicide, d. 1675.

but truly his patience is great; and he wishes he had a fair opportunity to give over.

Jno. Rushworth[8]

May 18th, 1647.
    For the Right Honble. Ferdinando, Lord Fairfax,
      at Denton, Yorkshire, these present.

By this time the soldiers were in a state of mutiny, and the whole force was drawn up on 10 June on Triploe Heath, seven miles south of Cambridge, to receive the Commissioners of Parliament headed by Skippon,[9] who had come with proposals which, if they had been offered earlier, would probably have been accepted, but which were now only regarded as a sign of weakness. Every attempt to read them to the men on parade was the signal for a pre-arranged and defiant outburst, so that the Commissioners were compelled to retire. On this the soldiers advanced as far as Royston in the direction of London, and from there they sent a menacing letter to the Parliament, which although signed by Fairfax amongst others, was generally supposed to have been the work of Cromwell.

The truth is that Fairfax had utterly lost control of the army that he was still supposed to command, as he was later himself to admit:

> From the time they [the Army] declared their usurped authority at Triploe Heath, I never gave my free consent to anything they did. . . . They set my name in a way of course to all their papers, whether I consented or not.

He was, however, still firm enough when action was required against the more extreme sectaries, as the Levellers were to find to their cost. Their leader, one Winstanley,[10] was anticipating Proudhon's doctrine, *La propriété, c'est le vol*, for he had declared that all landlords were breaking the eighth commandment: buying and selling were to be strictly prohibited, and any attempt to claim exclusive property in land was to subject the offender to branding with a hot iron. Neither Fairfax nor Cromwell had

---

[8] b. 1612, d. 1690. Rushworth was secretary to Sir Thomas Fairfax. He was also a historian of some note on account of his *Historical Collections* and sat in Parliament as MP for Berwick-upon-Tweed.

[9] Parliamentary general, d. 1660.

[10] A Leveller.

any sympathy with views such as this, and when the Levellers showed their hands in a rising in Surrey, Fairfax had no hesitation in crushing it.

Nevertheless, except in the field his authority had ceased to count, but there it was unshaken, as the outbreak of the Second Civil War was soon to prove. This was a particularly ill-organized affair, and to disperse most of the local risings was mere police work, but Cromwell had some hard fighting in South Wales before he turned north to crush at Preston the Scots, who were now in arms for the King while Fairfax dealt with an equally serious threat in Kent.

That county had remained steadily Roundhead during the first war, but it had now harked back to what a recent writer called 'its age-long tradition of spontaneous insurrection'. Several thousand Royalists gathered on Penenden Heath outside Maidstone, and were somewhat leisurely discussing their next move when Fairfax, with the main body of the New Model, fell upon them: he then drove them into Maidstone, and stormed the town. Lord Norwich, the Royalist commander, after a fruitless attempt to surprise London, managed to get some of his troops across the Thames into Essex, where he joined forces with Sir Charles Lucas, and shut himself up in Colchester, which Fairfax at once proceeded to invest. Here, he was once again to give evidence of his weakness of character whenever he came under the influence of a stronger man, in this case the bloody-minded Ireton.[11]

Wars, both civil and national, are inclined to become more bitter the longer they last, and the only other explanation for his behaviour on this occasion is that this one had soured Fairfax's nature. Provisions in Colchester soon began to run short, and when the starving women in the town begged permission to pass his lines, the only reply Fairfax made was to order his men to fire over their heads, and when this failed to deter them a threat was added to drive them back naked. On 27 August 1648 Colchester surrendered, and Fairfax then proceeded to act in a manner which was to constitute a permanent blot upon his character.

He had already refused to discuss terms, and had insisted upon unconditional surrender, so when this had taken place he summoned before him the three Royalist generals, that is to say Sir

[11] b. 1611, d. 1651. Signed the death warrant of Charles I and died of fever when besieging Limerick.

Charles Lucas, Sir George Lisle, and Sir Bernard Gascoigne. They were then told

> that after so long and so obstinate a defence they found it necessary to deliver themselves up to mercy, it was necessary, for the example of others, and that the peace of the kingdom might no more be disturbed in that manner, that some military justice should be executed; and, therefore that council had determined they three should be presently shot to death.

The three men were thereupon taken into the yard outside, where they found three files of musketeers ready to carry out these orders.

Lucas was shot first, and when he fell dead Lisle embraced his corpse. He then looked at the firing-party and suggested that they should come nearer, whereupon one of them said, 'I'll warrant you, Sir, we'll hit you', to which Lisle replied with a smile, 'Friends, I have been nearer you, when you have missed me.' This time, however, they were not to miss, and Lisle fell without speaking another word. It was now Gascoigne's turn, and he had already divested himself of his doublet when he was told that he had been reprieved. The reason for this sudden change of plan was that it had been discovered that Gascoigne was not a British subject at all, but a Tuscan who could hardly speak English: when Fairfax and his colleagues found this out, they were frightened that if they put him to death the Grand Duke of Tuscany Ferdinand II, might take a dim view of their proceedings with unpleasant consequences for them, so that, to quote Clarendon, 'their friends or children who should visit Italy might pay dear for many generations'. The Grand Tour was much in vogue in those days, so Gascoigne's life was spared.

After the Restoration a memorial was erected:

> To the memory of Sir Charles Lucas and Sir George Lisle by command of Sir Thomas Fairfax, General of the Parliament army, barbarously murdered.

Fairfax's daughter, who had married the Duke of Buckingham, applied to Charles II to have this inscription erased, but the King replied by ordering the lettering to be cut deeper.

This atrocity, so out of keeping with Fairfax's character, throws a strong light upon it, and Clarendon is undoubtedly right when he attributes it to the influence of Ireton: it was conclusive evidence of his tendency to be swayed by stronger men than himself where political decisions had to be taken.

In these circumstances it was hardly to be expected that he would take any steps to save the King's life, in spite of an appeal to him by the Prince of Wales—he was far too much under Cromwell's influence.

To General Fairfax and his Council of War in England
                    The Hague, January 13/23, 1648/9
We have no sources of information regarding the health and present condition of the King, our father, but the common gazettes which come into this country, our servant, Symons, whom we lately sent to present our humble respects to His Majesty, not having been able to obtain permission to to do so, or to see him. We have reason to believe that, at the end of the time assigned for the treaty made with His Majesty in the Isle of Wight, His Majesty has been withdrawn from that island, to Hurst Castle, and thence conducted to Windsor, with the intention of proceeding against him with more rigour, or of deposing him from the royal dignity given him by God alone, who invested his person with it by a succession undisputed, or even of taking his life; the mere thought of which seems so horrible and incredible that it has moved us to address these presents to you, who now have power, for the last time, either to testify your fidelity by reinstating your lawful King, and to restore peace to the kingdom—an honour never before given to so small a number as you—or to be the authors of misery unprecedented in this country, by contributing to an action which all Christians think repugnant to the principles of their religion, or any fashion of government whatever, and destructive of all security.

I therefore conjure you to think seriously of the difference there is in the choice you make, and I doubt not you will choose what will be most honourable and most just, and preserve and defend the King whereto you are by oath obliged. It is the only way in which any of you can promise himself peace of conscience, the favour and good will of His Majesty, the country and all good men, and more particularly of your friend,

Charles P.

Fairfax attended one meeting of the High Court of Justice but, when he found what was in the wind, to his credit he absented himself after that, but nothing more. His wife, a member of the Vere family, was made of sterner stuff. When the roll of the judges was called, and her husband's name was read out, she shouted from the gallery, 'He has more wit than to be here.' When, later on, Bradshaw,[12] the President of the Court, spoke of a charge of treason and other crimes exhibited against Charles by 'the people of England', she shouted again, 'It is a lie. Not a quarter of them. Oliver Cromwell is a traitor.'

It may not at first have been realized who had spoken these words, for Lady Fairfax and her friend Mrs Nelson, who had been with her on the former occasion too, had taken the precaution of disguising themselves in masks, but all the same the sensation was immense, and the soldiers were infuriated. They had been carefully picked from the extremists in the New Model, and their commanding officer, one Daniel Axtell,[13] was typical of the sort of soldier who was now coming to the fore. When he heard the interruption he appears to have shouted, 'Down with the whores!', or something to that effect, and commanded his men to fire into the gallery. Whether the order was understood to be conditional on further action on Lady Fairfax's part, or whether the soldiers, hardened as they were, drew the line at shooting down their Lord General's lady, who would seem by now to have been recognized, no shot was fired; and while they hesitated, the two ladies solved the problem by leaving their box. What is significant is that neither Bradshaw nor even Cromwell appears to have taken any subsequent steps to call her to account.

All the same a republican regime was instituted and the King was executed without Fairfax making any show of opposition: furthermore, in May 1649 he used his influence at great personal

[12] b. 1601, d. 1659. He was President of the Court which sentenced Charles I to death and he remained a republican during the Cromwellian regime. He was buried in Westminster Abbey, but his body was disinterred at the Restoration.

[13] Executed at the Restoration.

risk to help Cromwell to quell a dangerous mutiny of the troops: by the following year, however, he would appear to have had enough, and he made the proposal to invade Scotland an excuse for retiring into private life. Whitelocke, in his *Memorials*, gives an interesting account of a conference which then took place, and at which he was himself present:

Cromwell. My Lord General, we are commanded by the Council of State to confer with Your Excellency touching the present design of marching the army under your command into Scotland.

Fairfax. I am very glad of the opportunity of conferring with this committee about this great business of marching into Scotland, wherein I do acknowledge myself not fully satisfied as to the grounds and justice of our invasion upon our brethren of Scotland.

Lambert.[14] Will Your Excellency be pleased to favour us with the particular causes of your dissatisfaction?

Fairfax. My lords, you will give me leave with all freedom to say to you that I think it doubtful whether we have a just cause to make an invasion upon Scotland. With them we are joined in the National League and Covenant: and now for us contrary thereunto to enter into their country with an army, and to make war upon them is that which I cannot see the justice of, nor how we shall be able to justify the lawfulness of it before God or man.

Cromwell. I confess, My Lord, that if they have given us no cause to invade them it will not be justifiable to invade them, but if they have invaded us, as your lordship knows they have done, since the national covenant and contrary to it in that action of Duke Hamilton, which was by order and authority from the Parliament of that kingdom and so the act of the whole nation. . . . If these things are not a sufficient ground and cause for us to endeavour to provide for the safety of our own country and to prevent the miseries which an invasion of the Scotch would bring upon us, I humbly submit it to Your Excellency's judgement. . . . But

[14] b. 1619, d. 1694. Prominent Parliamentary general. He opposed Cromwell's assumption of supreme power, but at the Restoration he was banished to Guernsey.

there will be war between us I fear is unavoidable. Your
Excellency will determine whether it be better to have this
war in the bowels of another country or of our own.
Fairfax. If we were assured of their coming with their army
into England, I confess it were prudence for us to prevent
them; but what warrant have we to fall upon them unless
we can be assured of their purpose to fall upon us?
Harrison.[15] I think, under favour, there cannot be greater
assurance or human probability of the intentions of any
state than we have of theirs to invade our country, else
what means their present levies of men and money, and
their quartering soldiers upon our borders? It is not long
since they did the like to us, and we can hardly imagine
what other design they can have to employing their forces.

In spite of the very forceful arguments of his colleagues,
Fairfax continued to insist that his conscience would not permit
him to invade Scotland, and that he preferred to resign his
commission. This suited Cromwell very well as removing the
last obstacle out of his path.

Fairfax was now enjoying a pension of £5,000 a year, and on
this he lived quietly at Nunappleton during the Protectorate. He
had not, incidentally, done too badly out of the war, for quite
early in it he had been voted by Parliament £4,000 a year besides
a lump sum of £40,000 down. His relations with Cromwell would,
it seems, have deteriorated with the passage of time, and he was
closely watched by Thurloe's spies: the widening breach was in
no way healed when the Protector threw his son-in-law, the Duke
of Buckingham, into the Tower. With Cromwell's death Fairfax
came out into the open, and vigorously opposed Richard. The
culmination of all this was seen when Monk marched south, and
Fairfax, who was suffering from gout at the time, put all his
influence behind him: we are told that he 'became another man,
his motions so quick his eyes so sparkling, giving the word of
command like a general'.

There was little doubt by this time where his sympathies lay,
for Monk had not long taken up his residence at Drapers' Hall in

[15] b. 1606, d. 1660. Signed the death warrant of Charles I and was a
prominent Parliamentary general, but was later imprisoned for his
relations with the Anabaptists. He was executed at the Restoration.

London before he received a letter from Fairfax, together with a declaration from the county and city of York in favour of the return to their seats of what were known as the secluded members of the House of Commons, that is those who had been purged by previous regimes, and for a free Parliament. Support of this nature was just what Monk wanted, and on 18 February he replied to Fairfax to the effect that he was glad to say that 'the House hath condescended that their numbers shall be filled upp, and that all the writts shall shall issue forth for the electing of members'. Nothing was yet said about the re-establishment of the monarchy, but it was pretty clear in what direction Fairfax's thoughts— there can have been none about those of his wife—were tending. His father had died in 1648, and he was now head of his family, so in all these circumstances it is in no way surprising that he should have been chosen as one of the Parliamentary delegation to ask Charles II to return: he had, of course, succeeded to the Scottish barony of Fairfax of Cameron, but he was still frequently styled 'Sir Thomas' in the documents of the day.

Fairfax played no great part in public life after the Restoration, and died in 1671.

CHAPTER 4

MONTROSE

The personality of Montrose is not so easy to assess as that of some of the men and women who make their appearance in Colonel Dower's collection of letters, yet upon a grasp of it depends to no inconsiderable extent an understanding of more than one event in the Civil War. Admittedly in its earlier stages his career had been somewhat inconsistent and, as has been shown on an earlier page, this had probably rendered the Queen suspicious of him: he had even signed the Covenant, but it must be remembered that in those early days that document committed its signatories no further than to resist any religious innovations while stressing their loyalty to the throne. He soon, however, came to the conclusion that the King's opponents were going too far, and he thus summed up the situation as he saw it:

> And you, ye meaner people of Scotland . . . Do ye not know, when the monarchical government is shaken, the great ones strive for the garland with your blood and your fortunes? Whereby you gain nothing; but, instead of a race of Kings who have governed you two thousand years with peace and justice, and have preserved your liberties against all

domineering nations, shall purchase to yourselves vultures and tigers to reign over your posterity . . . The kingdom fall again into the hands of one who of necessity must, and for reason of State will, tyrannize over you. For kingdoms acquired by blood and violence are by the same means retained.

Certainly he did not become a convert to the King's religious views, for almost with his last breath he declared, 'Bishops, I am not for them. I never intended to advance their interests.'

From then onwards Montrose was continually pressing his master to allow him to make a diversion in Scotland. The Stuarts, however, with the notable exception of Charles II, were bad judges of character, and Charles preferred the advice of the in-constant and incompetent first Duke of Hamilton[1], which was contrary to that of Montrose, so it was not until 1644 that he was authorized to take the necessary action: had he been allowed to take it in the previous year, the war might have had a very different ending, for Leven's[2] invasion of England would probably never have taken place, and if the battle of Marston Moor had been fought at all, it might well have been a Royalist victory. Yet between September 1644 and September 1645, when he was defeated at Philiphaugh, he won a series of battles which, though on a smaller scale and in a less important theatre of war, have been compared with the Italian victories of Napoleon and Suvaroff.

Omelettes, however, cannot be made without breaking eggs, and Montrose's opponents were better propagandists than he. Much, for example, has been made of the alleged atrocities when the Royalists captured Aberdeen: what actually happened was that Montrose sent in a drummer under a flag of truce to ask the Provost to remove the old men, women, and children, but his emissary was promptly murdered. In these circumstances it was only natural that Aberdeen should be put to the sack, and the Roundhead propagandists flooded Scotland with stories of women slaughtered, though it is to be noted that their names were never given. It was very necessary to depict Montrose as a veritable monster of iniquity, in much the same way as Claver-house was held up to the obloquy of a future generation.

[1] b. 1606, beheaded 1649.
[2] The first Earl, d. 1661.

When Charles had surrendered to the Scots, it was obvious that he could no longer continue to support Montrose against them, so in May 1646 Montrose was ordered to lay down his arms, go to France, and await instructions. The King had made the best terms for him that he could, and they were that he should leave Scotland by 1 September in a vessel provided for him by the Estates: after that date his life would be forfeit. The more extreme Covenanters were furious when they heard of what appeared to them to be the easy conditions obtained by their enemy, and though they could not openly repudiate them, they were determined to annul them by secret treachery; so the ship provided for Montrose's voyage did not come into the port of Montrose until the last day of August, when her captain, a morose Covenanter, swore that he would not be ready to sail for another week. Montrose, however, had anticipated some such double-dealing, and had made the necessary arrangements with a Norwegian skipper lying off Stonehaven, who duly took him on board, and landed him safely at Bergen a few days later.

According to the King's orders Montrose went on to Paris, but he found no instructions awaiting him there—if they were ever sent they never came into his hands. It has been held that he played his cards badly in the French capital. Queen Henrietta Maria seems, indeed, to have become fully reconciled to him by now, and was certainly gracious to him, but she was much under Jermyn's influence, and his support was never forthcoming for any cause which might prove adverse to his own interests. In particular he kept the purse, and would allow no strange fingers in it. Furthermore, Montrose was accused of setting too high a price on his past services, while the publication of Wishart's narrative of his exploits, which might indeed have been postponed to a more favourable time, is said to have been seriously resented as likely to offend the more moderate Presbyterians to whom the Royalists were now turning for help. Contemporary gossip was running along these lines, and perhaps not entirely without reason.

Hyde, for example, who though by no means a whole-hearted admirer of Montrose, was always prepared to do justice to him, wrote of him at this period of his life:

[He] had not such a reception from the Queen of England, and

those who were in credit with her, as he thought the notable
services he had performed for the King had merited. The
truth is, he was somewhat elated with the good actions he
had done; which, upon his first coming to Paris, he caused
to be published in a full edition in Latin, dedicated to the
Prince of Wales; in which, as his own person, courage and
conduct was well extolled, so the reputation of all the rest
of that nation (upon whose affections the Queen at that time
depended) was exceedingly undervalued and suppressed;
which obliged the Queen and the Prince to look less
graciously upon him; which he could not bear without
expressing much disturbance at it.

He was then a man of *éclat*, had many servants, and more
officers, who had served under him, and come away with
him, all of whom he expected the Queen should enable him
to maintain with some lustre, by a liberal assignment of
monies. On the other hand, the Queen was in straits enough,
and never openhanded, and used to pay the best services
with receiving them graciously, and looking kindly upon
those who did them. And her graces were still more towards
those who were like to do services, than to those who had
done them.

Not that Montrose was not lionized in Paris, and Mazarin
offered him a command in the French army, but he was not
tempted; so he went to Prague where the Emperor, Ferdinand III,
not only received him most graciously, but promised him every
assistance in a new Scottish campaign. So Montrose retraced his
steps to the west, and at Tournai began to draw up plans with the
Spaniards, when the crushing defeat inflicted by Condé on the
Imperial forces at Lens rendered any active aid from that quarter
impossible. Montrose then returned to Brussels, where he at once
got in touch with Prince Rupert, who had newly arrived at The
Hague.

Sir
    Your Highness may justly think strange what should em-
bolden me to this freedom, never having done myself the
honour to have used the like before, nor being favoured with
your commands now to do it. But when your Highness shall

be pleased to know, that I was ever a silent admirer of yours, and a passionate affecter of your person, and all your ways, you will be pleased to allow me recourse to your goodness and generosity, and the rather that your Highness sees I am for the present at such distance, with all interests as no end but marked respect can now prompt me to it; which if your Highness shall do me the honour to take in good part, and command me to continue, I shall have, it will not harm the King, your uncles' service, nor what may touch your Highness, both in relation to those and their points, in either whereof I should presume to be able to do you some small service, so hoping your Highness will pardon the boldness, and take it from the true fountain. I shall only say, that I desire to be ever,

Sir, your Highness's most humble, faithful,
affectionate servant
Montrose

Brussells, 7th. Sept, 1648

Rupert returned a friendly answer, but regretted that his new duties as Admiral of the Fleet left him at present no time for an interview. In fact, Montrose was by no means *persona grata* with many of the exiles, for co-operation with the more moderate Presbyterians was the order of the day, and to them Montrose was anathema. In effect, Rupert was unwilling to commit himself too far at this stage, but Montrose refused to take no for an answer:

Sir

I had the honour to receive your Highnesses, by Sir John Urrie,[3] and was informed by him, likewise of all, your Highness committed to him, to deliver; to which I could not have failed, to have made an instant return, but that I was still upon my dispatch with their slow gamesters here, to have wait upon your Highness myself; which finishing draw to a little more length than I could have imagined, I am constrained humbly to crave your Highness pardon, to be

---

[3] A Scots mercenary who changed sides more than once during the Civil War. Executed 1650.

resolved of your commands, in this way; I must confess (as your Highness has perhaps heard) that it is my resolution, to return, for the Imperial court (tho' I never intended it, without being resolved, first to receive your commands, as the person's, in the world shall have greatest influence upon all my services) in regard there is nothing of honor amongst this stuff here, and that I am not found useful for his Majesty's service in the way to home, always if your Highness shall wish me engage or find a fair way for it or be to lay your rest at any stake, I entreat your Highness believe, that I have still so much invincible loyalty to his Majesty, and passionate respect to your own person, that I will abandon, all fortunes and advantages in the world, and rather hazard to sail by you, nor serve myself aside of all others, wherefore let you Highness be pleased, I may receive your commands freely, by your return, and I will study to forego all and dispose upon myself in everything accordingly, I make bold to do it, in this way because I wish not (if your Highness be pleased to think fit) that any should know what passes until I have first the honor to wait on your self which shall undoubtedly be after the return, at which time I hope to let your Highness see all is not yet gone but that we may have a handsome pull for it and a probable one, and either win it or be sure to lose it fairly; the pressingness of time makes me use this freedom, to which I shall add nothing, but a begging of your Highness pardon with a solemn vow, That I am, Sir,

Your Highness most humble faithful
affectionate Servant
Montrose

Brussell, 3rd. Decr., 1648.

Montrose was undoubtedly a gallant soldier, and a great leader of men, but he was not a very clear thinker—at any rate he did not excel at putting his thoughts into writing, and Rupert must have wondered what exactly this letter was about; but worse was still to come. In Colonel Dower's collection is another letter, also from Montrose to Rupert, which appears to make no sense at all: it is undated, but from internal evidence was obviously written before the King's execution.

Sir

If those people who pretend his Majesty's orders for me, and are to be directed hither as they profess, by the prince, be posted ere this come to your Highness hands, I shall not fail to attend you with all possible speed; otherways if they be not, your Highness would be pleased in an indirect way to dispose it so, as they may immediately be sent along, for it will concern much, that we know how their designs are composed and upon what string they touch that when I have the honor to wait on your Highness, we may with the more clearness cast our moulds, and know how to keep the better consort, with their train so that it will be much time gained altho' it may seem to retard it since notwithstanding I were with your Highness now, before you could resolve any thing it were necessary to find out their mine, that you might the better know how to labour yours, and until then the less they know of my faithful respects to your Highness or intentions towards his Majesty's service, it will be much the better for the more necessity they stand of men and the less certainty to have them, will still afford us the more freedom and greater square, to work, as for the present difficulties of your Highness shipping you need not doubt it, for there will be many ways found, for their entertainment, that they may still be kept in call, and since there be so handsome and probable grounds for a clean and gallant design if the measure be rightly taken I should be infinitely sorry that your Highness should be induced to hazard your own person or those little rests upon any desperate thrust, for while you are safe we shall find twenty fair ways to state our own selves and give them the half of the fear but if any thing else did behappen I should esteem myself the most unfortunate person in the world both for his Majesty's interest and your own person, always I will submit myself to your Highness better judgement and intreat you pardon this freedom which only proceeds from the entire and perfect respects of, Sir,

Your faithfulest and affectiontist Servant
Montrose

So matters would appear to have remained until news of the

King's execution reached the Royalist exiles: in the meantime Hyde states that Montrose remained in Brussels 'very privately, and as incognito'. There is, however, another account of his activities during this period which would have us believe that he was a suitor for the hand of Princess Louise, an elder sister of the future Electress Sophia of Hanover. However this may be, nothing came of Montrose's desires, while the lady, who became a talented artist, lived until 1709, when she died as Abbess of Maubuisson.

Of one thing there can be no question, and that is of Montrose's almost religious devotion to Charles I. When the news of the King's death reached him we are told that he fainted, and when he recovered he burst into passionate exclamations of grief, declaring that there was now nothing left for him in life. When reminded that there was still vengeance, he replied, 'It is so, and therefore I swear before God, angels, and men, that I will dedicate the remainder of my life to avenging the death of the Royal martyr, and re-establishing his son upon his father's throne'. This vow he then proceeded to embody in the following lines:

> Great, Good, and Just, could I but rate
> My grief with thy too rigid fate,
> I'd weep the world to such a strain
> As it should deluge once again;
> But since thy loud-tongued blood demands supplies
> More from Briareus' hands than Argus' eyes,
> I'll sing thine obsequies with trumpet-sounds,
> And write thine epitaph in blood and wounds.

The exact sequence of events after this is not too easy to follow but, apparently having failed to obtain an interview with Rupert, he applied direct to the new King, according to Hyde to know 'if His Majesty thought his attendance upon him might bring any prejudice to His Majesty; and if so, that he would send over the Chancellor of the Exchequer to Sevenbergh, a town in Flanders, where he was at present to expect him, and had matters to communicate to him of much importance.' Charles II had not the least desire to have Montrose at The Hague at that particular moment, though the last thing he wished to do was to offend him, for he was in negotiation with the moderate Presbyterians as well as with Argyll,[4] and Montrose's presence would only complicate

[4] The eighth Earl and first Marquis, b. 1597, executed 1661.

matters. So he told Hyde to go to see him, which Hyde was most unwilling to do, partly because he disapproved of the King's flirtation with those whom he considered to be Scottish rebels, and partly because he thought that Charles should bid Montrose 'very welcome, and prefer him before any other of that nation in his esteem'.

The meeting duly took place, but it would appear that the two men were not naturally sympathetic to one another. With all his virtues, Hyde was a good deal of a narrow-minded Englishman, with a dislike of other nations, which included the Irish and the Scots, while Montrose, great leader of men that he undoubtedly was, clearly lacked charm when it came to dealing with individuals. So nothing much came of their discussions, and Montrose went to The Hague after all. There Charles yielded to his wishes, and allowed him to go to Scotland: when he found that no useful purpose would be served by his action he sent a message of recall, but it never reached its destination, and Montrose was captured and executed.

The somewhat uneasy relations between Montrose and his fellow-Royalists reveals a basic weakness in the monarchist cause which has too often been ignored by historians, namely the national differences which existed between the royal supporters, and which were so prominent in the Jacobite movement in the following century—indeed they greatly contributed to its ultimate failure. No man, for example, could have been more devoted to Charles I and his son than Hyde, but he viewed the Queen with no favourable eye as a foreigner and a Roman Catholic, and the fact that Montrose was a Scot was clearly at the bottom of the failure of the two men to see eye to eye. When it came to the Irish they were regarded by English and Scottish Royalists alike, with the notable exception of Montrose, as quite beyond the pale —to be used when they could be of service, and then cast off. (The fact that Bonnie Prince Charlie had a slight Irish accent, derived from his early tutors, was often held against him by his English and Scottish supporters.) Occasionally the head of the House of Stuart at the time was able to enforce some sort of unity, but usually this was not the case, and the quarrels between the English, Irish, and Scottish supporters of the Stuarts played into the hands of their opponents for upwards of a century.

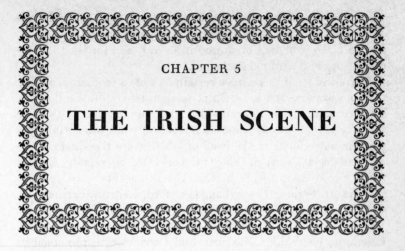

CHAPTER 5

THE IRISH SCENE

It would be impossible to exaggerate the influence of events in Ireland upon the Civil War in England and Scotland, and therefore it will be as well at this point to describe their background. While Strafford ruled across the Irish Sea, the discontented were afraid to lift their heads, but in 1640 he was recalled and lesser men took his place. Before long it became obvious that there was really no government in the country at all, while Britain herself was distracted by quarrels which were to end in civil war. Such being the case, Irishmen might well hope that a general uprising would shake off the English yoke, regain for them the lands lost by the various Plantations, and ensure full freedom for the Catholic religion. The elements of this rising existed both at home and abroad. In Ireland it found its leaders among the surviving members of the Celtic aristocracy such as Sir Phelim O'Neill, who regarded himself as head of the great house which had so long ruled in Ulster; Lord Maguire; and Rory O'More, whose family had been deprived of their property in Leix. Abroad there was a whole army of Irish soldiers in the service of Spain and the Empire, not least of them being Owen Roe O'Neill, and large numbers of priests and friars in the Irish colleges of Spain, Italy, and the Low

Countries. A union was now formed between these different elements, and while Rory O'More championed the cause at home, Father Luke Wadding organized it abroad, and sought the help of the Pope and Cardinal Richelieu.

In Ireland itself there was a certain lack of co-ordination among the conspirators, and an attempt to capture Dublin Castle by a *coup de main* failed to materialize; but by the end of October 1641, the north was in flames as a result of what was definitely a popular movement, at the head of which were the chiefs of the old Irish septs, such as The O'Conor Don. So rapidly did the rising spread that within a week the insurgents were absolute masters of Tyrone, Monaghan, Longford, Leitrim, Fermanagh, Cavan, Donegal, and Londonderry, with a part of Armagh and Down; while only a few forts, as well as the towns of Derry, Coleraine, Enniskillen, Lisburn, and Carrickfergus remained in the hands of the English settlers.

It would be idle to pretend that the rising was not accompanied by a number of revolting atrocities, but there was much to avenge, and what horrors did take place were the work of downtrodden and enraged peasants, and not of the deliberate policy of an allegedly civilized government as in the case of Elizabeth's commanders in the previous century. It is often stated that in more than one instance the Catholic clergy encouraged their flocks in the perpetration of these excesses, and it is to be feared that sometimes this was the case, for toleration of the opinions of others was not an outstanding characteristic of seventeenth-century clerics of any denomination; as the attitude of the Presbyterian ministers in Scotland also goes to show; on the other hand there were priests who, at the peril of their own lives, gave shelter to fugitive Protestants.

The actual number of people killed was probably not considerable—some three or four thousand slaughtered at the outbreak of the rebellion, and twice as many may have perished in ways less direct. What, however, admits of no doubt is the effect upon contemporary English and Scottish opinion: neither the number of the victims nor the manner of their deaths lost anything in the telling for propaganda purposes, while the blame was unanimously placed upon the Catholic Church, and both then, and for years afterwards, it became almost a dogma of the Protestant faith that the Catholics were plotting a general massacre of their opponent in all three kingdoms—the provocation which the Irish had so long received being conveniently forgotten.

The qestion at once arose as to how the rising was to be crushed, and Charles announced his intention of personally taking command of the army to be raised for this purpose. Such a solution did not, as may be imagined, suit Parliament at all, and its leaders replied that they did not approve of it. Their attitude was only natural, for if the King returned from Ireland at the head of a victorious army, they could expect short shrift themselves, as they were later to receive from Oliver Cromwell in similar circumstances. Some troops were, in fact, sent from both England and Scotland, but they did not effect very much. The Irish gradually gained possession of practically their whole country, and established what amounted to a provisional government at Kilkenny, though they still acknowledged Charles. By this time the King had raised his standard at Nottingham, and as both he and the Irish had a common enemy in the English Parliament, it was only natural that negotiations should take place between them.

To the Marquess of Ormonde

Charles R.

Right trusty and right well-beloved cousin and counsellor, we greet you well. Since our two Houses of Parliament here (to whose care at their instance we left it to provide for the support of our army in Ireland, and the relief of our good subjects there) have so long failed our expectation, whereby our said army and subjects are there reduced to very great extremities; we have thought good (for the preservation of our good subjects there) to resume the care of them again to ourself; and to the end that we may the better understand, as well the state of that our kingdom (as it is now reduced) as the cause of levying the arms that are at present there held against our authority; we have thought fit by these our letters to command and authorize you (the Lieutenant-General of our army there), with all secrecy and convenient expedition, to treat with our subjects (who have there taken up arms against us and our authority), and to agree with them for a present cessation of arms for one year, in as advantage-ous and beneficial a manner as you in your wisdom and good

affection to us (whereof we have had very good expressions)
shall conceive to be for our honour, and to conduce most to
our service; the particulars whereof we cannot prescribe
unto you, being we are not well informed of the true state
of our or their army or forces, or of the condition of the
country, or any other thing, whereupon to fix a judgement,
but shall remit the same entirely to you, promising hereby
in the word of a king, that we shall under our great seal
ratify and confirm whatsoever you, upon such treaty shall
conclude and agree unto, and set under your hand on our
behalf in this business; for which these our letters shall be
your sufficient warrant.

> Given at our court at Oxford, 23rd, April, 1643

The first Marquess of Ormonde was appointed Lord-Lieutenant
of Ireland by Charles on the following 13 November.

After some negotiation an armistice for one year on the basis
of the *status quo* was concluded on 15 September 1643, and in this
way the first period of the Irish rebellion came to an end. Immediately after this, Charles and Rupert began to see what armed
assistance they could get from Ireland, and two letters from
Ormonde to the latter are quoted on an earlier page. Particularly
was this the case after the beginning of the following year when
the Scottish army entered England in support of the Parliament,
but the great difficulty was that the mastery of the seas, as we
have seen in Ormonde's letter, was in the hands of the enemy,
and control of the sea-ports was at the best uncertain.

This vein runs through the King's correspondence with
Ormonde during the whole of the next year or two. For example,
on 9 January 1645 we find Charles writing from Oxford:

> You must take speedy order to provide all the shipping you
> may, as well Dunkirk, as Irish, bottoms; and remember that
> after March it will be most difficult to transport men from
> Ireland to England, the rebels being masters of the seas.

The importance of these western sea-ports goes far to explain
the King's annoyance at Rupert's surrender of one of the most
important of them, namely Bristol.

The impression has often been created that Charles did not

obtain any military assistance from Ireland, but this was not the case: from the conclusion of the Irish armistice about twelve regiments of foot and one of horse did cross the Irish Sea, and some of them landed in the south-west, while the majority were shipped across to Chester.[1] These reinforcements, useful as they were, cannot, however, be compared in importance with the Scottish army; in any event they had suffered severe losses at the battle of Nantwich in January 1644. Furthermore, we are told that their morale was lukewarm: there was no reason why it should have been anything else—and in some cases even suspect; while some units, according to one story, actually went over to the enemy during the fighting.

All the same, the King did not despair:

Oxford, February 27, 1645

Ormonde

The impossibility of preserving my Protestant subjects in Ireland by a continuation of the war, having moved me to give you those powers and directions, which I have formerly done, for the concluding of a peace there; and the same growing daily much more evident, that alone were reason enough for me to enlarge your powers, and make my commands in the point more positive.

But besides these considerations, it being now manifest that the English rebels have (as far as in them lies) given the command of Ireland to the Scots; that their aim is a total subversion of religion and royal power; and that nothing less will content them or purchase peace here, I think myself bound in conscience not to let slip the means of settling that kingdom (if it may be) fully under my obedience, nor to lose that assistance, which I may hope from my Irish subjects for such scruples as (in a less pressing condition) might reasonably be stuck at by me for their satisfaction.

I do therefore command you to conclude a peace with the Irish, whatever it cost, so that my Protestant subjects there may be secured, and my royal authority preserved. But for all this, you are to make me the best bargain you can, and

---

[1] A good many of these may, however, well not have been Celts at all, but were drawn from the units originally sent to put down the rebellion.

not to discover your enlargement of power till you needs
must; and though I leave the managing of this great and
necessary work entirely to you, yet I cannot but tell you,
that if the suspension of Poyning's Act[2] for such Bills as shall
be agreed on between you there, and the present taking away
of the penal laws against Papists by a law will do it, I shall
not think it a hard bargain, so that freely and vigorously
they engage themselves in my assistance against my rebels of
England and Scotland, for which no conditions can be too
hard, not being against conscience and honour. So I rest

Your most assured, constant friend
Charles R.

On 14 June 1645 occurred the battle of Naseby, which was
marked by the slaughter in cold blood when the fighting was
ended of such Irish soldiers and their womenfolk as fell into the
hands of the victors. It was a foretaste of what was to come at
Drogheda and Wexford, and was a link in that chain of atrocities
which in our own time have been associated with the Black and
Tans and the Provisional IRA. Undoubtedly the Roundheads
believed that they were only exacting retribution for the wrongs
which the Irish Protestants had suffered a few years earlier, and
in this belief they were encouraged by their spiritual advisers, in
whose creed toleration and forgiveness had no place. At the same
time, it cannot be denied that even a more moderate section of
English opinion regarded with disfavour the King's efforts to
recruit Irishmen for his forces, though why this should have been
the case it is difficult to understand. No objection seems to have
been taken on the score of their nationality to the employment
of Scots by the Parliament, and the Irish were equally the King's
subjects: indeed, in the following century the Hanoverian mon-
archs did not hesitate to use foreign mercenaries against the
Jacobites and the Americans who were their subjects. It was, too,
apparently all right for English troops to make war in Ireland,
but it was the worst of crimes for Irish troops to do the same thing
in England, The Irish, in short, were regarded as quite outside

[2] Poyning's Act had been passed in 1495, and it placed the Irish
legislature in complete subordination to England, for it provided that
all measures brough before the former must previously have received
the approval of the King and the English Privy Council. It was repealed
in 1782.

the pale, and a hideous legacy was being bequeathed to posterity.

Bewdley, June 18, 1645

Ormonde

The late misfortune which I have had makes the Irish assistance more necessary than before; and now the speedy performance of it is almost of as great importance as the thing itself; the which I most earnestly recommend to your wonted care and diligence. For if within these two months you could send me a considerable assistance, I am confident that both my last loss would be soon forgotten, and likewise it may (by the grace of God) put such a turn to my affairs, as to make me in a far better condition before winter than I have been at any time since this rebellion began, and (to deal freely with you) otherwise I am likely to be put to great straits.

This bearer, FitzWilliams, came recommended to me by my wife: what interest he hath in that country you will be better able to judge than I; they say very great, but certainly he is a man of great courage and perfect affections to my service; and as such, I confidently recommend him to you; but what charge to give him, or how to employ him, I leave to your judgement to do, as you shall find best for his service, who is

Your most real, constant friend
Charles R.

I desire you to send me speedy and frequent advertisements to what port to direct the ships for transporting your men.

To add to the King's difficulties Ormonde, though a paragon of Cavalier loyalty, was, as has been shown, a diehard Protestant, to whom the mere idea of toleration for Catholics was anathema. Charles must have realized this, and he not unnaturally came to the conclusion that he might get more out of the Irish if he made use of a negotiator who held different views. Unfortunately his choice, bad judge of character as he generally proved himself to be, fell on the newly created Earl of Glamorgan, son of the Marquess of Worcester.

Whether Glamorgan was a charlatan or merely a wishful thinker is not easy to decide. By his own account he would seem

93

at one time or another to have invented almost everything that was then unknown, from flying to perpetual motion, for he satisfied himself that he had designed a wheel which, by a mere distribution of weights, would go on revolving to the end of time. He is also claimed in some quarters as one of the many fathers of the steam engine. However, more recent examination of Glamorgan's record of his own discoveries has left the impression that they consisted of pipe-dreams, with seldom even an attempt to produce a working model.

It was only natural that a man with so fertile an imagination should early have come to the conclusion that he could solve the Irish problem—an infinitely more baffling one than any in the field of mechanics—but it was peculiarly unfortunate that in addition to deceiving himself he should also have deceived the King, though how far Charles was deceived must be a matter of opinion, for as early as 27 December 1644 he is found writing of Glamorgan to Ormonde: 'His honesty or affection to my service will not deceive you; but I will not answer for his judgement.' Carte considered that his great qualities were 'destroyed by an extreme bigotry in point of religion; a narrow capacity, a want of judgement, and an unmeasurable degree of vanity'. Various causes delayed his arrival in Dublin until August 1645, when the King's affairs were fast going to ruin anyway.

Yet it is hard to blame Charles in his extremity for allowing this highly plausible emissary to see what he could do in the way of persuading his fellow Catholics to produce those ten or twenty thousand soldiers who might just conceivably turn the scale in what was now a hopeless conflict in England: even a chance in a thousand may be worth trying when the alternative offers no chance at all.

Hereford, June 23 1645

Glamorgan

I am glad to hear that you are gone to Ireland; and assure you that as myself is in no ways disheartened by our late misfortune, so neither is this country, for I could not have expected more from them than they have now freely undertaken, though I had come hither absolute victorious, which makes me hope well of the neighbouring shires, so that (by the grace of God) I hope shortly to recover my late loss with

advantage if such succours come to me from that kingdom
which I have reason to expect: but the circumstances of time
is that of the greatest consequence, being that which is now
the chiefest and earnestliest recommended to you by

Your most assured, real, constant friend
Charles R.

Glamorgan, being a wishful thinker if ever there was one,
should have been given more precise instructions. Most, if not
all, of his alleged credentials were forgeries of a blatant kind. That
he had verbal or informal written instructions, which could be
discovered, as indeed they were, can be granted, and no doubt
he acted loyally in what he thought were the King's best interests;
but the vital documents, as shown to the Confederate Irish and
the Nuncio, were either forged throughout, or more probably,
written on prepared blanks bearing the King's sign manual.

Cardiff, July 31, 1645

Ormonde

It hath pleased God, by many successive misfortunes, to
reduce my affairs, of late, from a very prosperous condition
to so low an ebb as to be a perfect trial of all men's integrity
to me, and you being a person whom I consider as most
entirely and generously resolved to stand and fall with your
King, I do principally rely upon you, for your uttermost
assistance in my present hazards: I have commanded Digby
to acquaint you at large with all particulars of my condition;
what I have to hope, trust to, or fear; wherein you will find,
that if my expectation of relief out of Ireland be not in some
good measure and speedily answered, I am likely to be
reduced to great extremities.

I hope some of those expresses I sent you since my
misfortune by the battle of Naseby are come to you, and am
therefore confident that you are in good forwardness, for the
sending over to me a considerable supply of men, artillery,
and ammunition: all that I have to add, is, that the necessity
of your speedily performing them, is made much more
pressing by new disasters; so that I absolutely command you
(what hazard soever that kingdom may run by it) personally
to bring me all the forces of what sort soever you can draw

from thence, and leave the government there (during your absence) in the fittest hands, that you shall judge, to discharge it; for I may want you to command those forces which will be brought from thence, and such as from hence shall be joined to them.

But you must not understand this as a permission, for you, to grant to the Irish (in case they will not, otherwise have a peace) anything more, in matter of religion, than what I have allowed you already, except only, in some convenient parishes, where much the greater number are Papists, I give you power to permit them to have some places, which they may use as chapels, for their devotions, if there be no other impediment for obtaining a peace; but I will rather choose to suffer all extremities, than ever to abandon my religion and particularly to either English or Irish rebels, to which effect I have commanded Digby to urge to their agents, that were employed hither, giving you power to cause deliver or suppress the letter, as you shall judge best, for my service.

To conclude, if the Irish shall so unworthily take advantage of my weak condition, as to press me to that, which I cannot grant, with a safe conscience, and without it, to reject a peace, I command you, if you can, to procure a further cessation; if not, to make what divisions you can, among them; and rather leave to the chance of war, between them and those forces, which you have not power to draw to my assistance, than to give my consent to any such allowance of Popery, as must evidently bring destruction to that profession, which by the grace of God, I shall ever maintain, through all extremities.

I know, Ormonde, that I impose a very hard task upon you, but if God prosper me, you will be a happy and glorious subject; if otherwise, you will perish nobly and generously, with and for him, who is,

Your constant, real, and faithful friend
Charles R.

During the next few weeks matters went from bad to worse for the King: Rupert surrendered Bristol to Fairfax, and Montrose was beaten at Philiphaugh. The situation in Ireland, too, was changing, and not for the better. In the field an outstanding victory was won by Owen Roe O'Neill at Benburb, which was very definitely a triumph for the Old Irish, while even more important was the arrival of Giovanni Battista Rinuccini, Archbishop of Fermo, as the Nuncio of Pope Innocent X, with a supply of money, arms and ammunition which went far to heighten the influence of his sacred character. The Nuncio was not concerned with politics but with the interests of the Catholic Church, and he was by no means disposed to let a heretical prince have orthodox help at a low rate. In these circumstances the King determined to see what could be done by an appeal to the Pope himself:

Most Holy Father

So many and so great proofs of the fidelity and affection of our cousin the Earl of Glamorgan we have received, and such confidence do we deservedly repose in him, that Your Holiness may justly give faith and credence to him in any matter, whereupon he is to treat, in our name, with Your Holiness, either by himself in person or by any other. Moreover, whatever shall have been positively settled and determined by him, the same we promise to sanction and perform. In testimony whereof, we have written this very brief letter, confirmed by our own hand and seal; and we have in our wishes and prayers nothing before this, that by your favour we may be restored into that state, in which we may openly avow ourself

Your very humble and obedient servant,
Charles R.

At our court at Oxford, October 20the, 1645

By this time Ormonde, loyal as he was to the King, was becoming what today would be termed frustrated. Both on religious and political grounds he was mistrustful of the Nuncio, and he now protested against the diminution of his own powers in favour of Glamorgan. Charles accordingly endeavoured to pacify him:

January 30, 1646

Ormonde

I cannot but add to my long letter, that upon the word of a Christian, I never intended that Glamorgan should treat

97

anything without your approbation, much less without your
knowledge. For besides the injury to you, I was always
diffident of his judgement (though I could not think him
so extremely weak), as now to my cost I have found him;
which you may easily perceive by a postscript in a letter of
mine to you, that he should have delivered to you at this
his last coming into Ireland; which if you have not had, the
reason of it will be worth the knowing, for which I have
commanded Digby's service, desiring you to assist him.

And albeit I have too just cause, for the clearing of my
honour, to command (as I have done) to prosecute
Glamorgan in a legal way; yet I will have you suspend the
execution of any sentence against him until you inform me
fully of all the proceedings. For, I believe, it was his mis-
guided zeal, more than any malice, which brought this great
misfortune on him and us all. For your part you have in this,
as in all other actions, given me such satisfaction, that I mean
other ways, more than by words, to express my estimation
of you. So I rest

Your most assured, constant, faithful friend
Charles R.

The recruitment of Irish soldiers to serve in England was
hardly stimulated by a resolution of Parliament refusing quarter
to them, and in any case it is not easy to see what claim Charles
had upon the spontaneous loyalty of what, thanks to English rule,
was already well on the way to becoming 'the most distressful
country that ever yet was seen'. However, Glamorgan had been
induced to sign a secret treaty granting all the points in dispute,
of which a copy was most unfortunately found on the Catholic
Archbishop of Tuam, who, while taking part in the siege of Sligo,
had been killed in a sally of the garrison. Digby scented the
possible damage and denounced the treaty, an action which met
with the whole-hearted approval of Charles: Glamorgan was put
under arrest, but the damage was already done, for the Parliament got hold of the secret treaty and ordered it to be published.
Thus without obtaining one soldier from Ireland as a result of
Glamorgan's mission the King incurred unspeakable distrust in
England: even Ormonde saw no hope in the circumstances, and
he decided to surrender Dublin to the Parliamentary forces which

were on their way to Ireland, preferring, as he put it, 'English rebels to Irish rebels'. Accordingly, when Colonel Michael Jones[3] arrived with several thousand Roundheads, he put this plan into execution on 28 July 1647, and himself left the country.

[3] He had earlier won the battle of Rowton Heath.

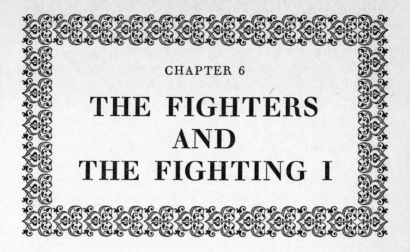

CHAPTER 6

THE FIGHTERS
AND
THE FIGHTING I

As one reads through Colonel Dower's collection of letters one cannot help being struck by the gradual change which took place in the character of the war at it progressed, or rather in the attitude of the participants towards it: something has been said about this on an earlier page, but the matter must be discussed in somewhat greater detail.

If there are many fallacies current as to the political aspect of the Civil War, those with regard to its tactics are no less numerous. The royal army is often believed to have consisted mainly of cavalry, under the command of Prince Rupert, who invariably executed a headlong charge upon their opponents from which, as often as not, they failed to return until the day had been lost in other parts of the field. As for the Roundheads, from being for the most part 'old, decayed servingmen and tapsters', as Cromwell called them at the beginning of the struggle, they evolved into a force as immortal in history as the Old Guard of Napoleon. There is some truth in these popular conceptions, but it is by no means the whole story. It is first of all necessary to forget all modern notions of a cavalry charge, along with memories of an avalanche of mail-clad knights in the great days of chivalry.

Richard Coeur de Lion is as far removed from the seventeenth century in this respect as the 21st Lancers at Omdurman, the Light Brigade at Balaclava, or Murat galloping into action at Austerlitz with his cavalry thundering behind him, rank after rank, their horses 'stretched out like greyhounds'.

All this must be forgotten if any mental picture is to be formed of the mounted troops of Rupert's and Cromwell's day. Shock tactics were a thing of the past. Gunpowder and small arms had scared them off the field. The seventeenth-century trooper was a clumsy, lumbering figure, in a stout, buff coat, with breastplates, a heavy iron helmet with bars across his face, and further encumbered with pistols or, in the case of the dragoon, a weighty and unhandy musket, advancing at a slow trot towards his enemies (with frequent halts to fire volleys at them), and finally coming in among them, sword in hand, at a speed that can never have amounted even to a canter.

In effect, even the greatest captains of the preceding century had thought of cavalry as mounted infantry. From the days of Gonsalvo de Córdoba, more than a hundred years before, the Spanish infantry with its hedgehog of pikes, had been supreme on the battlefields of Europe, and earlier still the lessons of Agincourt were hardly reassuring to the advocates of shock tactics. Rupert did much to change all this, and the legend of his reckless charges doubtless owed its rise to the fact that his practice of charging home was an innovation learnt from Gustavus Adolphus. The horses, too, would have been small to modern eyes, but when their riders' equipment is taken into consideration it is clear that they must have been expected to carry twenty to twenty-five stone. The English Civil War contributed not a little to the development of the cavalry arm, for Cromwell was too good a soldier not to apply the lessons which his opponents had taught him; a generation later the charge of the Polish lancers outside Vienna broke the Ottoman power for ever, but it was Rupert at Edgehill who set in motion that cavalry revival which John Sobieski was notably to exploit.

With Cromwell's character as a man and as a statesman we are not concerned here, but in the early days of the Civil War there can be no question but that it was as a soldier and an organizer that he rendered the greatest service to the cause of the Parliament. Two letters to the Deputy-Lieutenants of Essex bear this out:

August 1st., 1643

Gentlemen

The time I was absent from Nottingham this bearer was forced to borrow of the Mayor of Nottingham £100 for the payment of the three companies belonging to your counties, besides shoes, stockings, shirts, and billet money, which I promised should be repaid. I receiving no money out of your counties where withal to do it, I can but refer it to your considerations; for I think it is not expected that I should pay your soldiers out of my own purse.

This is the sum of his desire who rests your truly loving friend.

Oliver Cromwell

August 6th., 1643

Gentlemen

You see by this enclosed the necessity of going out of your old pace. You sent indeed your part of the 2,000 foot; but when they came they as soon returned. Is this the way to save a kingdom? Where is the doctrine of some of your county concerning the trained bands and other forces not going out of the association?[1] I wish your forces may be ready to meet with the enemy when he is in the association.

Haste what you can; not your part only of 2,000 foot, but I hope 2,000 foot at least Lord Newcastle will advance into your bowels. Better join when others will join, and can join with you, than stay till all be lost; hasten to our help. The enemy in all probability will be in our bowels else in ten days; his army is powerful. See your men come and some of your gentlemen and ministers come along with them, so that they may be delivered over to those shall command them, otherwise they will return at pleasure. If we have them at our army we can keep them.

From your faithful servant

Oliver Cromwell

Territorially the basic weakness of the King's position was that London was in the possession of his enemies, and he never really had a chance of reversing this state of affairs once he had rejected Rupert's request to make a dash on the capital after the battle of Edgehill. Elsewhere the balance of forces depended very largely

[1] The Eastern Association.

upon the attitude of the local magnates. In the north the running was for a time made by the Royalist Earl of Newcastle, though the Fairfaxes, father and son, had a considerable backing in the West Riding of Yorkshire, especially in the clothing towns. The alleged devotion of Lancashire to the Stanley family was soon exploded, and the entry of the Scots into the war finally turned the balance in the North of England in favour of the Parliament, the issue being clinched at Marston Moor.

Wales was almost entirely Royalist, but it was a poor country in those days, though a good recruiting-ground. The Eastern and Home Counties, dominated by London, inclined to the Parliament, as did Buckinghamshire, Essex, and East Anglia, largely because of their long-standing Puritan traditions. There is also to be taken into account the influence of the Parliamentary leaders such as John Hampden and Arthur Gardiner in Buckinghamshire; Warwick in Essex; and Lord Saye in Oxfordshire, though the last-named had to face the rivalry of the Earl of Northampton. Except for a few towns the west was on balance for the King. Regionalism and the influence of the county families in the seventeenth century possessed an importance which it is not easy to understand to-day.

As the war progressed there was a change in the morale of the two parties, as the letters of the leading combatants clearly show, that of the Roundheads as steadily rising as that of the Cavaliers fell. The attitude of Cromwell, for instance, in the following letters, is markedly different from that in the two written in 1643 and already quoted. The first is one written after Marston Moor, for among those killed in that battle was a young relative of the future Lord Protector, and the latter's letter to the boy's father, a Colonel Walton, is interesting both for an account of the fighting (as seen through Cromwell's eyes) and for the manner in which he broke the news of the young man's death:

Deere Sir

It's our duty to sympathize in all mercyes; that wee praise the Lord together, in chastisements or tryalls that we may sorrowe together. Truly England, and the Church of God, hath had a great favor from the Lord in this victorie given unto us, such as the like never was since this War begun. It had all the evidence of an absolute Victorie obtained

by the Lord's blessing upon the godly partys principally.
Wee never charged but we routed the enemie. The left
Winge, which I commanded being our owne horse, saving a
few Scottes in our reere, beat all the Prince's horse. God
made them as stubble to our swords. We charged the Regiments of foote with our horse and routed all wee charged.
The particulars I cannot relate now; but I believe of twenty
thousand, the Prince hath not four thousand left. Give glory,
all the glory, to God.

Sir, God hath taken away your eldest sonn by a cannon
shott. Itt broke his legge. Wee were necessitated to have itt
cutt off, whereoff hee died.

Sir, you know my tryalls this way, but the Lord supported
me with this, that the Lord took him into the happiness
wee all pant after and live for. There is your precious child,
full of glory, to know sinn nor sorrow any more. Hee was a
gallant younge man, exceedingly gracious. God give you his
comfort. Before his death hee was soe full of comfort, that
to Franke Russell and my selfe he could not expresse it, itt
was so great above his price. This he sayd to us. Indeed itt was
admirable. A little after he said, one thing lay upon his spirit; I
asked him what that was; he told mee that it was that God had
not suffered him to be noe more the executioner of his enemies.

Att his fall, his horse being killed with the bullett and as
I am informed three horses more, I am told he bid them open
to the right and left, that he might see the rogues runn.
Truly he was exceedinly beloved in the Armie of all that
knew him. But few knew him; for he was a precious yonge
man, fitt for God. You have cause to bless the Lord. Hee
is a glorious saint in heaven, wherein you ought exceedingly
to rejoyce. Lett this drinke up your sorrowe. Seeing theise
are not fayned words to comfort you; but the thing is soe
real and undoubted a truth, You may doe all things by the
strength of Christ. Seeke that, and you shall easily beare
your tryall. Lett this publike mercy to the Church of God
make you to forgett your private sorrow. The Lord be your
strength; soe prays

Your truly faythfull and loving brother
Oliver Cromwell

July 5th. 1644.

Naseby found Cromwell in an even more ebullient mood, for after the battle had been fought and won he wrote to William Lenthall, the Speaker of the House of Commons, as follows:

Sir

 Beinge commanded by you to this service. I thinke my selfe bound to acquaint you with the good hand of God towards you and us. Wee marched yesterday after the King whoe went before us from Daventree to Haverbrowe,[2] and quatered about six miles from him. This day we marched towards him. Hee drew out to meet us. Both armies engaged. Wee, after three houres fight, very doubtfull, att last routed his Armies, killed and tooke about five thousand, very many officers, but of what quality wee yet know not. Wee took also about two hundred carrages, all hee had, and all his gunnes, being twelve in number, whereof two were demiecannon, two demie culveringes, and (I thinke) the rest sacers. Wee persued the enimie from three miles short of Haverb. to nine beyond, even to sight of Leic[r] whether the King fled.

 Sir, this is non other but the hand of God, and to him alone belongs the glorie, where in none are to share with him. The Generall[3] has served you with all faythfullness and honor, and the best commendations I can give him is that I dare say hee attributes all to God, and would rather perish than assume to himselfe; which is an honest and a thrivinge way, and yett as much for bravery may be given to him in this action as to a man. Honest men served you faythfully in this action, Sir they are trusty. I beseech you in the name of God not to discourage them. I wish this action may begett thankfulnesse and humility in all that are concerned in itt. Hee that venters his life for the libertye of his countrie, I wish hee trust God for the libertye of his conscience and you for the libertyee hee fights for. In this hee rests, whoe is

Your most humble servant
Oliver Cromwell

June 14th., 1645

[2] Harborough
[3] Sir Thomas Fairfax

On the Royalist side there was a great deal more self-reliance and not so much dependence on the kind services of the Almighty. Take, for example, the following letter from the Earl of Northampton to Prince Rupert:

Sir

The rebel forces are gone from Daventry into the further quarters of Northamptonshire, where they have received some opposition at a place called Wellingborough, by the rising of the country there on his Majesty's behalf. On Monday last, at night, they seized upon one Mr. Grey, the clerk of the peace for that county, living in Wellingborough, and carried him prisoner to Northampton. At which the town ringing their bells, the country people thereabouts came in, and on Tuesday there was a great skirmish, most part of yesterday, in which old Sawyer, one of the committee, and their captain, was slain, and their men dispersed. But about four that day, in the afternoon, came the rebel forces from Northampton, and over came the country, and have plundered all Wellingborough town, and are carrying the goods to Northampton.

The rebels are not yet returned, but lie scattered in the town and thereabouts by forties and fifties in a company; so that if there could be but three hundred dragoons with a regiment of horse, sent, it would not only disperse them, but encourage the country to rise on his Majesty's behalf against them, and I am confident, to a considerable number. Otherwise those parts will be much ruined, to his Majesty's great prejudice.

This being all I can send your Highness, I am, Sir, your Highness's

Most humble servant
Northampton[4]

Banbury
December 28th., 1642.

The Royalist commanders were by no means 'yes-men', and could be outspoken when they thought the occasion required, as

[4] The second Earl. Killed at the battle of Hopton Heath.

may be seen by a letter Henry Wilmot[5] wrote to Rupert under
date of December 1st., 1642:

> May it please your Highness
>
> Even now I received a command from your Highness to
> be to-morrow night at Wantage where I shall not faile to
> obey any commands laid upon mee according to my power,
> but give me leave to tell your Highness that I think myself
> very unhappy to be employed upon this occasion, being a
> witness that (at other times) in the like occasions troops are
> sent out without any means of forecast or design or care to
> prepare or quarter the troopes when they are abroad, if I
> had any place to quarter my horses I should wait on your
> Highness this night at Oxford, to-morrow it will be too late,
> so that I shall obey your Highness in being at Wantage and
> there expect information how to behave myself, which I
> shall not fail immediately to see done. Soe most humbly
> kissing your Highness hand I rest your Highness most
> humble and most faithful servant
>
> Wilmot

Even the King himself was not spared advice as to the way in
which he should conduct the war, for the Marquess of Winchester is
found writing from Basing House under date of 2 December 1642:

> Most Gracious Sovereign
>
> Since by command your Majesty's forces at Basingstoke
> are drawing off, and the enemy now lying within less than
> ten miles of this place, I conceive this Castle to be in apparent
> danger, and cannot be long kept without some assistance from
> your Majesty's army; for from this county no relief is to be
> expected it standing for want of your presence and some
> authority to command it divided in itself.
>
> If this house be any way considerable for your Majesty's
> service and advantage, be pleased to take it into your
> consideration and protection least I shall be necessitated to
> leave it to the will of the enemy. I refer more particulars
> to the relation of the bearer in case your Majesty will
> vouchsafe to him.

[5] Royalist general. Victor of the battle of Roundway Down.

My duty and affection to your Majesty's service occasions this address from

Your Majesty's most faithful
and Loyal subject
Winchester[6]

In the Royalist camp credit for a victory was given where it was due, and did not have to be shared with the Almighty. When Rupert had captured Cirencester he received the following letter from Wilmot:

Sir

There is no servant you have, does rejoice more in the happy victory you have had: I hope the same success will attend you in all your actions. Before this business the enemy did press very strong upon our quarters towards Buckingham here, but I believe now we shall be very little troubled with them; I was in hope by this time to give your Highness an account that your horse here were well recruited, but I am now in little hope of doing it at all, we not having received one penny to that as yet. Sir, Sir Thomas Aston being not here I have sent my letter into Dorsetshire to command his person hither but I have not heard (as yet) from him, when I do, I shall obey your Highness commands, so most humbly kissing your Highness hand I rest, Sir,

Your Highness most humble
and most faithfull servant
Wilmot.

Oxford, 27th., March, 1643

A few other letters in Colonel Dower's collection give a good idea of the way in which the war was run on the Royalist side in its earlier years:

Charles R.

Right entirely beloved Nephew, we have this day by Sir James Aunion written to you to hasten hither to us, leaving in our county of Stafford such competent forces as may secure

[6] The fifth Marquis.

the same; and least that our letter should miscarry, we have thought it necessary, considering how much it imports us to use our utmost endeavours to repel the great forces of the rebels now before Reading, by this express to second our former letters sent to you, desiring you to use all possible diligence to come away with so much of the forces there as may with the security of those parties be spared: And so we bid you heartily farewell,

Given at our Court at Oxford, the 16th of April, 1643
To our most deere and most
entirely beloved Nephew Prince Rupert
Palatine Generall of our Cavallery

Nephew

I thank you for your often advertisements, desiring you to continue them; I like very well of your resolutions: only I shall remember you how fit it is to hinder Waller's recruiting by all possible means, it being of more importance to my affairs to ruin him than the taking of any towns, which bring to your consideration I rest

Your loving uncle and faithful friend
Charles R.
Oxford, 20 July, 1643

Charles R.

Most dear Nephew

We greet you well. Since our last to you we have received certain advertisement that the Earl of Essex is come near Aylesbury, that he hath five hundred fresh horse come to him from London, that the Lord Gray is joined with him, and that Sir William Waller is come thence previously with a very good strength also [word indecipherable] the rebels Forces.

Besides this we have lately sent the Lord [word indecipherable] Regiment into Hampshire which makes Us second our former letters to desire you to hasten hither as many of the Horse with you as may be possibly spared. And we bid you heartily farewell. Given at our Court at Oxford the 24th. day of July, 1643.
You shall do well to hasten your business as much as may

be and remember to restrain plundering that all may go for
the Army and not for particular benefit.

C.R.

Nephew

The General is of opinion that we shall do little good
upon this town, for they begin to countermine us, which
will make it a work of time, wherefore he is of opinion,
(to which I fully concur) that we should endeavour to fight
with Essex as soon as may be, after we have gotten our
forces together, which I hope will be to-morrow those from
Bristol being already come; the greatest care will be, to meet
with him before he can reach the hedges: now if this be
your opinion, as it is ours (which I desire to know with all
speed) I desire you to do all things in order to it, that no
time be lost, so I rest

Your loving Uncle and most faithful friend

Charles R.

Matson 5 Sept 1643
    10 Morning

May it please your Highness

This morning his Majesty having received intelligence
that the enemy is marching towards us upon both sides of
the water did command me to write unto your Highness to
request your Highness that you would be pleased instantly
to send orders unto all your troops of horse who have this
day orders to march that they stir not from the place where
this night they lodge until they receive further directions:
in the mean time his Majesty will strive to obtain certain
intelligence, and upon your advertisement where you this
night lodge his Majesty will inform your Highness of all that
passeth, this presumption I beseech your Highness to pardon in

Your Highness's

most humble and faithful

servant

Arth. Aston

Reading, 21 Nov. 1643

I desire you to come hither that

we may advise what to do. C.R.

To his Highness Prince Rupert these humbly present.

111

Nephew

I suppose you will like this dispatch much better than the last by Persons, it will also give you assurance that the Yorkshire Petitions answer will be according to your desire: I am glad to find by your letter, which I received yesterday by Tomkins, that you are hopeful to be of a considerable strength shortly, which indeed was one of the motives that has caused this change of Orders, the chief being that you may be a security for Oxford, in case Essex should draw hither whilst we are seeking a revenge upon Waller: for the rest I refer you to this other letter.

So I rest
Your loving uncle and most
faithful friend
Charles R.

Oxford, 4 Ap. 1644

The reference to the Yorkshire Petitioners is to the pressure being exercised by the northern Royalists for help now that the Scots had entered England. As has been shown on an earlier page, Rupert was sent north in the spring of 1644 to retrieve the situation, and in particular to raise the siege of York. At first he was singularly successful, for he compelled the Parliamentary forces before Newark to capitulate, and then captured Stockport, Bolton, and Liverpool, as well as relieving Lady Derby at Lathom House.

A letter written about this time (the exact date is in dispute) from Goring to Rupert shows pretty clearly that the King's generals did not keep their grievances to themselves:

Sir

I have sent your Highness a copy of my Lord Digby's letter and the King's answer to the Prince and my answer to him, by which your Highness will see that I have no manner of certainty in any thing is promised me from Court and that they will rather distract all the King's business than suffer me to enjoy the benefit of your Highness favour or have this army or county, governed by any body but themselves, if only I had the affront in it I assure you faithfully, Sir, I should not have thrown down my burthen at this time, but when I can make it evidently appear that those which have procured this affront upon me have done nothing in the King's service since they came, but bring distractions into it, I will never be subject to those that will rather the King's service than not ruin me.

That which troubles me extremely is to have so faithful a servant removed from you at this time, but if I could have remained useful to your service I should have endured their opposition longer, but what assurance can I ever have of his Majesty's favours when it is in the power of these people to carry him point blank against his former orders, in earnest, Sir, I value so much the promises I have given you and the reasons of them in this particular, that I will never while I breathe submit to the Prince's council, and if I can not have your gift of the command of the council of the West ratified I will pray for the King but never take any command in his service more, I am very confident the King will find hereafter the difference between those he affronts and those he cherishes so much, wheresoever I am I shall be ready to serve where I may do it with my honour, and in the meantime there is nothing I preserve more in my heart than a tender passionate affection to your service and a resolution through the whole course of my life to perish rather than fail in being

Your Highness Most humble faithful and most
obedient Servant
George Goring

Meanwhile the King was writing to Rupert congratulating him on his successes:

Nephew

First, I must congratulate with you for your good successes, assuring you that the things themselves are no more welcome to me than that you are the means. I know the importance of supplying you with powder, for which I have taken all possible ways, having sent both to Ireland and Bristol, as from Oxford this bearer is well satisfied that it is impossible to have at present: but if he tell you that I may spare them from hence, I leave you to judge, having but thirty-six left;

but what I can get from Bristol (of which there is not much certainty, it being threatened to be besieged), you shall have.

But now I must give you the true state of my affairs, which, if their condition be such as enforces me to give you more peremptory commands than I would willingly do, you must not take it ill. If York be lost, I shall esteem my crown little less, unless supported by your sudden march to me, and a miraculous conquest in the South, before the effects of the northern power can be found here; but if York be relieved, and you beat the rebel armies of both kingdoms which are before it, then, but otherwise not, I may possibly make a shift (upon the defensive) to spin out time, until you come to assist me: wherefore I command and conjure you, by the duty and affection which I know you bear me, that (all new enterprises laid aside) you immediately march (according to your first intention with all your force to the relief of York; but if that be either lost, or have freed themselves from the besiegers, or that for want of powder you cannot undertake that work, you immediately march with your whole strength to Worcester, to assist me and my army; without which, or your having relieved York by beating the Scots, all the successes you can afterwards have most infallibly will be useless to me.

You may believe nothing but an extreme necessity could make me write thus to you; wherefore, in this case I can noways doubt of your punctual compliance with

Your loving uncle and faithful friend
Charles R.

Ticknell, June 14, 1644

Hardly can Rupert have received the King's letter of congratulation than he and Newcastle were defeated at Marston Moor on 2 July, and the north was lost to the Royalists. In consequence Newcastle departed to the Continent, where in due course he received the following letter from the King:

Charles R.

Right trusty and entirely beloved cousin and counsellor, we greet you well. The misfortune of our forces in the North, we know, is repented as sadly by you, as the present hazard of the loss of so considerable a portion of this our kingdom deserves: which also affects us the more, because in that loss so great proportion falls upon yourself, whose loyalty and eminent merit we have ever held, and shall still, in a very high degree of our Royal esteem.

And albeit the distracted condition of our affairs and kingdom will not afford us means at this present to comfort you in your sufferings, yet we shall ever retain so gracious a memory of your merit, as when it shall please God, in mercy, to restore us to peace, it shall be one of our principal endeavours to consider how to recompense those that have, with so great affection and courage as yourself, assisted us in the time of our greatest necessity and troubles; and, in the meantime, if there be anything wherein we may express the reality of our good intentions to you, or the value we have of your person, we shall most readily do it upon any occasion that shall be ministered; and so we bid you heartily farewell.

Given at our court at Oxford, the 28th day of November, 1644

> By His Majesty's command
> Edw. Nicholas

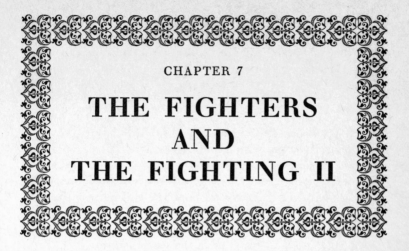

CHAPTER 7

THE FIGHTERS
AND
THE FIGHTING II

With the loss of the battle of Marston Moor, the Royalist sun began to set, and before long there was a marked decline in Royalist morale, but none of this was immediately noticeable, for in the west fortune was favouring the King, who was driving the Earl of Essex before him. Indeed, this had been obvious all the autumn, for on Christmas Day 1644 Hopton wrote to Rupert:

> May it please your Highness
> I have enclosed a relation of the state of affairs here now the enemy is retreated out of Somersetshire. I shall fall to settling of business here about Bristol, and the garrisons thereto belonging, of which I shall give your Highness a frequent account, something I am bold to write in cypher, which Mr. Secretary Nicholas his cypher that I hold with him will unfold. I humbly rest,
> Your highness
his most humble servant
Ralph Hopton
> Bath, Dec 25th., 1644

Nephew

I have given order to the Sherif of Oxford for Horses as
you have desyred, being of the same mynde now, as, I was
this Morning, for I hould it most requisit for my service that
you follow the Rebells at least as far as Derby or Nottingham
etc: if you fynde they advance before you towards Manchester or Cheshire; whether, then, you will follow them
your self or not, I leave you to judge; but I desyre, they
should be followed with a considerable strength; for otherwise, I much aprehend that they may loose me all those
Counties, not without hazard to my L. Newcastells Armies,
whose assistance and advyce I hope you will not want in this
business: In all this, I show you but my wish & opinion yet
no ways to prescrybe you, but freely to leave you to your
own judgement, as being upon the place: I rest

Your most loving Oncle
and faithfull friend
Charles R.

Oxford, this Monday 23 Jan
betweene 6 & 7 at Night

Charles endeavoured to take advantage of his improved position
in the West by writing himself to Essex:

Liskeard, August 6, 1644

Essex

I have been very willing to believe, that whenever there
should be such a conjuncture as to put it in your power to
effect that happy settlement of this miserable kingdom (which
all good men desire), you would lay hold of it. That season
is now before you, you having it at this time in your power
to redeem your country and the crown, and to oblige your
King in the highest degree (an action certainly of the
greatest piety, prudence, and honour), such an opportunity
as, perhaps, no subject before you hath ever had, or after
you shall ever have; to which there is no more required, but
that you join with me, heartily and really, in the settling of
those things which we have both professed constantly to be
our only aims. Let us do this: and if any shall be so foolishly
unnatural as to oppose their King's, their country's, and

118

their own good, we will make them happy (by God's
blessing), even against their wills.
The only impediment can be want of mutual confidence;
I promise it you on my part, as I have endeavoured to
prepare it on yours, by my letter to Hertford from Evesham.
I hope this will perfect it, when (as I here do) I shall have
engaged to you, on the word of a king, that you, joining
with me in that blessed work, I shall give both to you and
your army such eminent marks of my confidence and value,
as shall not leave a room for the least distrust amongst you,
either in relation to the public or yourself, unto whom I
shall then be
Your faithful friend
C.R.
If you like of this, hearken to this bearer, whom I have
fully instructed in particulars, but this will admit of no
delay.

Essex forwarded this letter to the Parliament, observing that it
was his business to fight, not to negotiate, but he proved singularly unsuccessful at it. On 31 August 1644 his army, which he
had previously deserted, capitulated at Lostwithiel, and Charles
foolishly allowed the men to go home after the confiscation of
their arms. Had he wished, he could have imposed far harsher
terms, and his moderation robbed him of the fruits of his most
complete victory.

About the same time the future regicide, Colonel John Hutchinson, was writing to 'Sir John Digby and the rest of the gentlemen at Newark':

Gentlemen
If that respect and care you express to this Town and
country were the right way, it would be much happiness
to both; as for your threats to this poor town we have
already had experience of your malicious endeavours to
execute that mischief which you now threaten against it;
but God restrained that time both the rage of your cruel
hearts and the power of your devouring element; and I trust
will still do the same for us.
I never engaged myself in this service with any respect

to the success of other places, though the kingdom were
quiet by our forces except this place, (which I trust God
never will permit) yet I would never forsake that trust and
charge which I have in my hands till that Authority which
honoured me with it shall command it from me, and if God
suffer the place to perish I am resolved to perish with it,
being confident that God at length will vindicate me to be
a maintainer and not a ruiner of my country.

Your servant
John Hutchinson

Nottingham, March 26th., 1644.

As we have seen, among the ablest but most difficult generals
on the Royalist side was Lord Goring. He is commonly dismissed
by historians as a debauchee, and there is, indeed, little doubt that
he was a hard drinker, but there is all the difference in the world
between a hard drinker and a drunkard: equally, if he had no
other claim to distinction, as his detractors would have us believe,
than an excessive devotion to the bottle, he would hardly have
proved himself so outstanding a cavalry commander in wartime.
His real weakness was that he was a brilliant individualist and was
at once unreliable, unpredictable, self-seeking, and quarrelsome.
As has been shown on an earlier page, when the New Model
Army was obviously about to take the field and the King had
concentrated north of Oxford an adequate army with which to
confront it, Goring was pressing to be allowed to resume his
independent command in the west. He was to pay for this attitude
a few weeks later on the field of Langport.[1]

About this time Charles decided to place his eldest son as far
from danger as he possibly could, and as the Royalists of the west
had planned an association of their counties, on the analogy of the
Roundhead Eastern Association, to encourage and direct their
labours the Prince of Wales was sent to hold his court at Bristol,
and with him as advisers went Hyde, Capel, Culpepper and
Hopton.

---

[1] A hostile contemporary wrote of him:
None had less regard than he
To justice, honour or integrity;
And cast in truth as men more honest thought
An odium on the cause wherein he fought.

May it please your Highness

I know not how my letters arrive with you, but this is the third I have written to you since I came from Bridgwater, in which I have given you an account of the state of this county, and of the levies here, which truly are advanced so well, that I am confident the King will have a very noble army from these parts; and if the civil business of these parts be attended, and prosecuted with that vigour and authority, as it may be, truly great things may be done.

I have already given you an account of the several garrisons, which I think are in the best condition, and the best fortified in England; and if your Highness gives directions for the regulating and reconciling those differences and contradictions in commissions, which I mentioned to you in my last, this county will be happy.

Since I wrote, that is on Sunday morning last, has arrived at Dartmouth a ship with two hundred barrels of powder, and at Falmouth there are great (very great) quantities of match and muskets, and pistols, arrived. I have given directions for drawing a good proportion of all to Bristol, by Barnstaple, and have likewise written to Charles Gerrard, to appoint some persons to receive his powder at Ilforde Come from whence he may have it at Swansea in one tide. I expect an answer from him to-morrow night, at Barnstaple, which I go to give direction for the constant transportation of all that ammunition which I have directed to be sent thither, for I would not venture too much at a time.

I have made two contracts, both which the Commissioners of the county have undertaken to make good, with two merchants of this city, who are gone six days into France: the one is to bring two hundred and the other is to bring three hundred barrels of powder; and they have promised that both shall arrive within twenty days after their going from hence; for I much fear Cullimore will not perform.

I hope to be at Bristol, or where the Prince is (I would were in these parts, for I hear the plague hath driven from Bristol), within four days. From whence I shall able your Highness again with many particulars, which

121

I had not now leisure to convey to you in cipher; and when I shall be most glad to receive any counsels from you, which shall be obeyed by no man with more cheerfulness and alacrity than by, Sir,

Your Highness's most obedient servant

Edward Hyde

Exeter, this 21st. of May, 1645

In the following letter, also to Rupert, there is a good deal of wishful thinking when the real facts of the situation are taken into account:

May it please your Highness

I take all the joy in the world in your good success the God of Heaven bless you. Sir Thomas Fairfax continues his Siege at Sherborne, the new foot that came from London came to him Monday night; they are in number seventeen hundred: here are seventeen old foot of your regiment come from them: there are five hundred horse come to Bath from Sherborne, they quartered last night at Phillips Norton; they talk that they are going to assist the Scots. (Sir, this inclosed came for your Highness last night and was open by the Governor of Guddrit Castle, that that the bearer was to say by word of mouth, was this) that they must be speedily relieved for they want victuals; powder and bullet they have enough, but if they are not suddenly relieved tis lost; the Governor sends your Highness this word that three thousand foot and two thousand horse would ruin their army.

The landing of the Irish is confirmed by several hands, but not so great a number, commanded by Colonel Fitzwilliam. From London this news comes that Montrose is advanced into England with fifteen thousand horse and foot: from the West I hear nothing. When your Highness letters come from Oxford I will speedily send them you.

Sir, I am very well pleased my little Captain Osborne did so handsomely, and his hurt only a mark of honour. We are settling the garrison according to your Highness orders; I hear from gentlemen that come from Wales hitherways that the King is still at Ludlow; Sir, what intelligence I receive I shall present you with all possible speed having as

great inclination to serve you as any person in the world
being eternally obliged

Your Highness

most obedient servant that honour you
with my heart and soul

H. Hawley

Bristol this
13th. August 1645

Such unjustified optimism may well have tended at first to
persuade Rupert that the military situation was better than it
was, but the Royalists in the west were soon overtaken by events.
Fairfax forced Sherborne to capitulate on 15 August, and on 23
August he appeared before Bristol: on 11 September Rupert
surrendered that city to him.

CHAPTER 8

THE EXILES

The scene now shifts to the Low Countries—there are no letters
in Colonel Dower's collection either from or to Charles I once he
had passed into the keeping of the Scots—and to the exiles there,
of whom the most notable was the Prince of Wales. His appointment in the west of England had not been a success, for he
found the generals quarrelling, the exchequer empty, and the
troops hopelessly undisciplined. By March 1646 it had become
obvious that peace was only possible on terms of unconditional
surrender, so the Prince with about three hundred followers
sailed from Pendennis Castle to the Scilly Isles. From there he
went to the Channel Islands, but he was driven out of Jersey by
the Parliamentary men-of-war, and in June he joined his mother
at the French Court—a step which his father had said should only
be taken in the last resort, and of which Hyde thoroughly disapproved.

For the next two years the Prince was a cipher at his mother's
exiled Court, and had no part in public affairs; but in the spring
of 1648 the English and Scottish Presbyterians united with their
old Royalist enemies to throw off the yoke of the army, which,
to quote Sir Arthur Bryant, 'had subordinated every authority in

the kingdom to the rule of force, and reduced its former master Parliament to a tiny band of members of its own way of thinking'. Risings took place all over the country, while a section of the Parliamentarian fleet mutinied and sailed over to Holland, where the Prince of Wales joined it at Helvoetsluys. However, before putting to sea he addressed letters to potential supporters in England, of which the following is a specimen:

> To the Mayor and Corporation of Kingston-upon-Hull
> Helvoetsluys, July 17, 1648

Trusty and well-beloved, we greet you well. We conceive it to be our duty to lay hold of all means that may probably conduce to the restoring of the King our royal father to his liberty and just rights, the redeeming of the whole kingdom from those heavy pressures which now lie upon it, and the settling of a well-grounded and happy peace. And it having pleased God to move the hearts of so many of the seamen to return to their natural obedience to the King, that now a great part of His Majesty's own navy royal . . . are under our command.

. . . We have therefore thought fit to invite you to partake with us and all the well-affected people of the kingdom . . . in our undertaking . . . by a reasonable declaration of yourselves against that arbitrary and lawless power of the sword, which oppresses the whole kingdom Which, if you shall do, we assure you and the whole town of a full pardon and indemnity for all that is past, and our just protection of all your ships and goods.

Unfortunately the risings in England proved abortive, for they were suppressed piecemeal by Fairfax and Cromwell, so the Prince was unable either to rescue his father from Carisbrooke, relieve the starving Royalist garrison of Colchester, or bring the Parliamentary fleet to action. For a short time he did, indeed, blockade the mouth of the Thames, but in September 1648 he was compelled through shortage of victuals to return to the Low Countries.

> To Prince Rupert
> May it please your Highness

The prince hath received your letter and hath commanded
me to return his thanks to your Highness for your greate
care and he is confident your Highness will meet with no
interruption in whatsoever you find necessary to be done,
by any Acts of the States, for he hath received advertisement
this morning that the Prince of Orange [word torn out] to
the Hague, and that he will be here by 12 of the [word torn
out] and likewise that 4 of the States are likewise appointed
to attend his Highness in this place, and then to go to the
Earl of Warwick with some message.

All shall be done that is possible in order to the fireships
and the procuring of an addition of strength to the fleet,
to the which it is hoped the presence of the Prince of
Orange will contribute very much. For the commission for
Captain Jordan I will take care to give your Highness a
speedy account, as soon as my Lord Culpepper and Mr.
Jonge (neither of whom are yet come hither) agree, in whose
hands all those transactions and commissions are: and I make
no question that Captain Fordayne in whose affection and
conduct the Prince hath a great confidence, will [six words
illegible].

Mr. Mortaigne hath delivered your Highness command to
me concerning the foot soldiers here, with which I have
acquainted the Prince, and directly shall be presently given
to find out the merchant and treat with him, but by reason
so many of the Prince's attendants are yet behind (for his
Highness came not in the last night till 9 at night attended
by very few) we have not such information in that particular
as is necessary, however if Dr. Goffe (who would be the best
instrument) come not this morning, I will find some other
way to move the Merchant. All other commands your
Highness shall vouchsafe to me, shall be punctually obeyed
by

Edward Hyde
Brill

Oct. 1, 1648

To Prince Rupert

Since the receipt of your Highness's letter the last night by
Sir William Vaughan, Mr. H. Hurry acquaints my Lords

that my Lord of Warwick is come nearer to you with his whole fleet. There is nothing here left undone, that we can possibly think of; yesterday morning upon your Highness first intimation of Trump's indisposition, my Lord Treasurer visited the Prince of Orange, and spoke frankly with him of the whole state of the Fleet, and remembered him of the promise upon the first arrival of it, that there should be 24 hours allowed us, and desired his Highness to give him privately his advice what we were to do.

After long and free discourse (of which I only give your Highness the relation) the Prince directed my Lord to come to him again this morning and then advised him that Sir William Boswell should presently apply himself to the States General, and signify in the Prince's name, that the Fleet is now ready to be gone, and therefore that he desires according to the Laws and customs of Nations that since his Fleet came first in, and the other be kept 24 hours after.

This Sir William Boswell hath done, and is this afternoon to attend them again, and we do believe as much will be done as they dare: I cannot believe this drawing near of Warwick is out of purpose to fight, but of design upon the advice of the revolted Frigate to corrupt your men, and it is possible that strategm may fail, though I fear in his posture the letter to the captain of the Frigate would produce but a small effect. I believe your officer will be disappointed in making his provisions at Amsterdam for the former defects if he depend upon the Massocria victual, for we have agreed for the whole quantity that is left; which is near enough for the new month but more pork than beef, though we conceive both very good: I have writ to Capt. Ulbert (whom Sir Wm. Vaughan tells me your Highness hath sent thither) that he only purchase that victuals, but not offer to pay for it, because he have it upon credit, and so that 5,000 guilders may find other provisions. The powder and match is likely ready, and shall come with the beef and the pork with all possible haste. I am now sending an express to Amsterdam to hasten it. The credit for that proportion of victual is all we could get among the Merchants of Amsterdam, but if the Fleet were once out, we should have more credit with them, in the mean time God knows what shift we shall make for money.

I presume the Duke of York is by this time at the Brill,
and I hope in better humour than he hath been. I dare
promise your Highness upon my credit with you, that you
will find Sir John Berkelly passionately devoted to serve,
and you may safely trust him, in any thing he undertakes
to do. I know I need not recommend my Lord Hopton to
your particular kindness, for your Highness knows him a
person of excellent courage and virtue; yet pardon me for
exhorting you to take him into more than your ordinary
favor; and give him occasion to believe you do so,
and you will find a faithful return from him. You have a
very good work in hand, yet with the advantage, that as you
shall receive great honour if it succeed, so if it miscarry, it
is evident no other person living could have done more. God
preserve your Highness.

Sir

Your Highnesse

most obedient servant

Edw: Hyde

Hague the 19th. of Nov^r.
Thursday 5 of the clock in the afternoon

At this point it is necessary by way of explanation of the relations between the Royalist exiles and their Dutch hosts to say
something of the internal politics of the United Provinces, which
for some years were marked by the clash between two opposing
systems of government, that is to say between the advocates of
the sovereignty of the States of the several Provinces and those
of that of the States General of the Union: by the former it was
indeed denied that the States General possessed any of the attributes of sovereignty at all. The Federal Assembly represented the
Republic in the eyes of the outside world, but it had no authority
save what was delegated to it by the seven sovereign Provinces
acting in accord: it could not coerce the Provincial States or take
action in opposition to their wishes. Had such a theory been
pushed to its extreme limits all government would have proved
impossible, but in practice it was corrected by the existence of
two strong, though antagonistic, influences.

One was the extensive executive power vested in successive
Princes of Orange, and by their own outstanding abilities, no less

than by virtue of the offices they filled, the Stadtholders William I, Frederick Henry, and William II exercised an authority which was strong enough at critical moments to override opposition. The other influence was that of the predominant Province of Holland, which bore more than half of the financial burden of the Union, and provided the greater part of its fleet. The States of Holland jealously guarded and vigilantly asserted their independence and privileges, while their control of the purse gave them an almost irresistible weight in the formulation of the policy of the Republic. As a not unnatural consequence of this conflict of powers it had twice, in 1618 and 1650, been necessary to settle the question of supremacy between Holland and the Generality by the sword, but the recent imprisonment of Jacob de Witt and five companions in the castle of Loevestein by William II seemed to have tilted the balance of favour of the House of Orange.

The last weeks of 1648 found the Royalist exiles in Holland whistling to keep their courage up. Early in December we find Hyde writing to Rupert from The Hague in an optimistic vein regarding the progress of events in Ireland, though what he had to be optimistic about it is not easy to see, and later in the month he was forced to admit that the attitude of the States was by no means helpful. Meanwhile Rupert was at Helvoetsluys with the ships that had left the Parliament service, and on two or three occasions he was compelled to repress mutinies, in one of which he found it necessary to throw seamen overboard by the strength of his own arms.

May it please your Highness

This day about eleven o'clock as I came from Anver, I had an inkling that there was a fellow come to town to arrest the *Charles*, the Captain had timely notice of it, and put himself upon his defence, the officer with two men with him came to the ship side, required to come in, and upon refusal showed his order upon the shore, and then retired into a house, whither I sent Sir John Mennes and Sir William Vaughan who told him the Captains had all order from your Highness to let none aboard their ships in your absence, and gave them a little money, and so I hope they are gone in good humor.

Sir John Mennes (whom I do desire to give his orders in

all things concerning the sea) hath ordered the *Charles*, to
make ready to go out into the roads as soon as she can, and
the *Blackmore Lady* and *Thomas* to put off towards the midst
of the channel here in the Sluice and to keep good water,
and for the business itself I think it were expedient that
his Highness the Prince of Wales took notice to the States
of this attempt and prayed them that if they will take upon
them a judicature between him and his father's subjects in
this clear case of pressing ships for his service yet that they
would not be so unkind as to arrest his ships, but that his
highness would rather answer their actions or Sir William
Boswell in the King's name.

Sir, your Highness sees how there grows daily more and
more need of your Highness presence here especially at this
time to get all things ready not to lose the next spring, for
there is great hope it may serve you for this wind and rain
clear all the ice, and if the wind chance to turn favourable
against the time do rise it may be a great opportunity, and
such as at this time of year is rare to be had the tides with
the wind are now higher here than they were in the [word
missing] of the spring, I humbly rest,

Your Highness his

most humble faithful servant

Ralph Hopton

Hellfort Sluice, Janry, 4th., 1649.

While these and similar bickerings were taking place the
Prince of Wales had an attack of smallpox: while he was con-
valescing at the Court of his brother-in-law, William II of Orange,
news reached him from England that Cromwell and the army
chiefs were about to put his father upon trial for his life. At
once the Prince wrote to the rulers of Europe asking for their
intercession, and he even, as we have seen, sent a letter to his
father's gaolers. This appeal was further reinforced by a blank
sheet of paper with the Prince's signature at its foot, which he
sent for Cromwell and his associates to fill up with any conditions
they chose to impose upon him in return for his father's life, but
the appeal was in vain, and on 30 January 1649 Charles I was
executed.

Colonel Dower's collection of letters to all intents and purposes

ends with the death of Charles I. It is, however, interesting to
note the part that, for the short remainder of his life, the Prince
of Orange played in his affairs, for we find him advising his
brother-in-law to accept Presbyterianism in the same spirit that
Charles's grandfather, Henri IV, had declared that Paris was
worth a Mass. Shortly afterwards, the Royalist cause suffered a
further blow in the death of William II of Orange, who had not
only helped it with money, but had also done much to counteract
the leanings of the Dutch republicans towards their English co-
religionists.

The last letter in Colonel Dower's collection is from Charles II
to Rupert, and is dated from Paris, where he was staying on a
visit to his mother, 22 March 1660:

My dearest Cousin

I am so surprised with joy in the assurance of your safe
arrival in these parts, that I cannot tell you how great it is,
nor can I consider any misfortunes or accidents which have
happened, now I know your person is in safety, if I could
receive the like comfort in a reasonable hope of your brother's:
I will not tell you how important it would be to my affairs,
when my affection makes me impatient to see you, I know
the same desire will incline you, after you have done what
can be only done by your presence there, to make what haste
to me your health can indure, of which I must conjure you to
have such a care as it may be in no danger.

I have sent Colonel Owen whom you know to be a very
honest man, to do you such service as you shall direct him.
Mr. Anthony will write to you more at large of all things, so
that I will say no more to you at present, only to assure you
I shall be very impatient till I see you, that I may myself
tell you with how much kindness I am,

My dearest Cousin
Your most affectionate Cousin
Charles R.

For my dear cousin
Prince Rupert

In a little over two months Charles was back in Whitehall—King
of England *de facto* as well as *de jure*.

INDEX

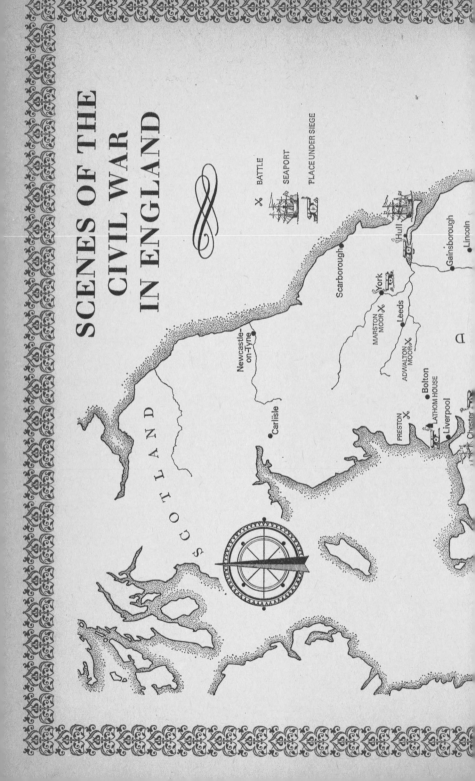

SCENES OF THE
CIVIL WAR
IN ENGLAND

✗ BATTLE

SEAPORT

PLACE UNDER SIEGE

SCOTLAND

Carlisle

Newcastle-on-Tyne

Scarborough

York

MARSTON MOOR ✗

Leeds

ADWALTON MOOR ✗

Hull

Gainsborough

Lincoln

PRESTON ✗

LATHOM HOUSE

Bolton

Liverpool

Chester

D